# Light

## Exploring the Energy You See

DEVELOPED IN COOPERATION

WITH

**MONTSHIRE MUSEUM OF SCIENCE**
NORWICH, VERMONT

Copyright © 1995 by Scholastic Inc.      All rights reserved. Published by Scholastic Inc.      Printed in the U.S.A.
ISBN 0-590-27738-3
1 2 3 4 5 6 7 8 9 10      09      01 00 99 98 97 96 95 94

## THE PHYSICAL WORLD IS GOVERNED BY THE PROPERTIES AND INTERACTIONS OF MATTER AND ENERGY.

# Light

Light, the form of energy responsible for vision, interacts with matter in a variety of ways and can be changed to other forms of energy.

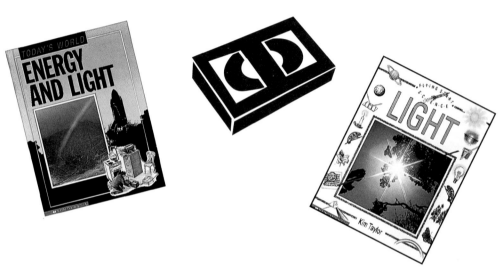

## Light can be reflected, refracted, scattered, or absorbed by matter.

## Light can change to other forms of energy.

## *Think Tank: Lighting a Space Station* Exploration Lab

# Turn On the Light!

Wham! "Ouch!"

Have you ever bumped into something in a dark room? Have you ever thought about why you can't see anything in a dark room, and why turning on the light makes it possible for you to see? What exactly happens inside your eyes once the lights go on? And why does flipping a switch on the wall make the light go on? And . . .

The questions could go on and on. Light is amazing. You can't hold it in your hand; it doesn't weigh anything. You can't trap it and store it, but plants can. All day long, the sky is bright with light that doesn't cost you a penny. But if you want light after dark, it's going to cost you.

## What do you know about light?

Thinking about light is a little like thinking about breathing. Both are such basic parts of your life that you've probably never thought much about them. Still, you probably know some things about light. Work with your class to make a list of what you already know.

## What do you want to know?

Make a second list with your class. This time, list questions you have about light. You could start your list with a question about the picture: What causes a rainbow to form in the sky?

## How will you find out?

You're going to work in teams to do the hands-on explorations in this unit. You and your partners will discover many of the answers to your questions. You'll also share information discovered by other teams in your class, and by other scientists.

## Using scientific methods:

Look at the table of contents. Each lesson title is a problem you're going to solve. Each problem you solve will help you solve the ones that come after it. In each exploration lesson, you and your class will use scientific methods to solve each problem:

• You'll make a *hypothesis* – a prediction – about possible answers to the problem.

• You'll do a *hands-on exploration* – sometimes two of them – that will help you test your hypothesis.

• You'll *record data* you collect.

• You'll *draw conclusions* from your data.

• You'll *compare* your conclusions to those of other teams in your class.

• You'll *apply* your conclusions to your own life.

The Video Mystery will help you get started. You're going to be taken to the scene of a mystery. You'll use clues from witnesses to help your class solve it.

# Where Does Light Come From?

Look out the window of your classroom. The sunlight you see has just finished a very long trip—about 150 million kilometers (93 million miles) from the sun to your eye. The most surprising fact about that trip is that it only lasted about eight minutes. <u>Light</u>—the form of energy that lets you see—always travels at an amazing speed. Besides the sun, what are some other sources of light energy?

## Exploration:
## Identify light sources.

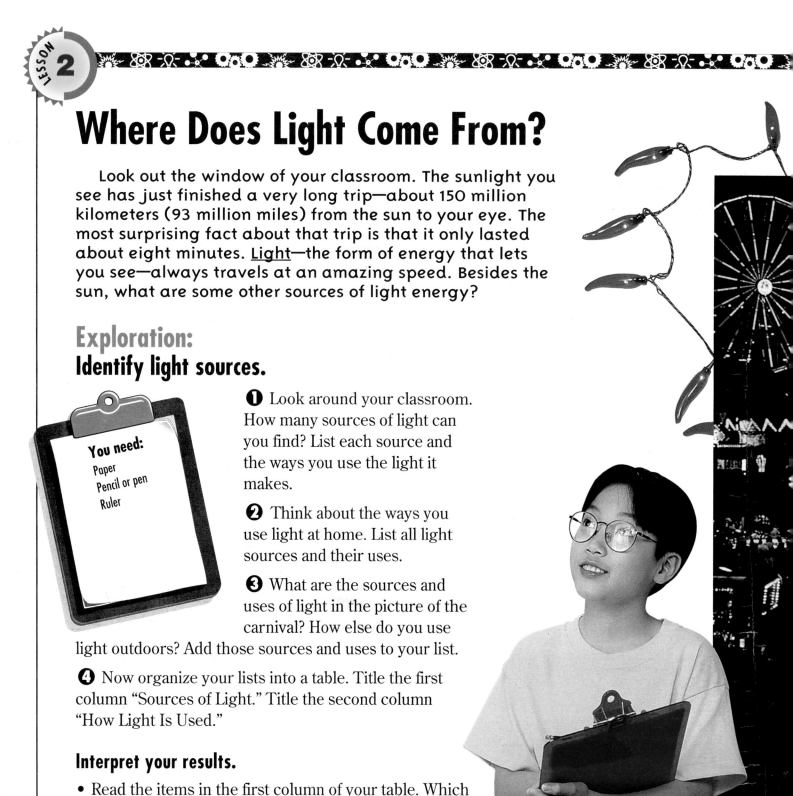

**You need:**
Paper
Pencil or pen
Ruler

❶ Look around your classroom. How many sources of light can you find? List each source and the ways you use the light it makes.

❷ Think about the ways you use light at home. List all light sources and their uses.

❸ What are the sources and uses of light in the picture of the carnival? How else do you use light outdoors? Add those sources and uses to your list.

❹ Now organize your lists into a table. Title the first column "Sources of Light." Title the second column "How Light Is Used."

### Interpret your results.

• Read the items in the first column of your table. Which items could be classified as natural sources of light? Which could be classified as artificial—that is, light made by humans?

• What is the most common use of light? How often do you use light for entertainment?

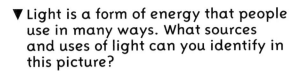

▼ Light is a form of energy that people use in many ways. What sources and uses of light can you identify in this picture?

## Exploration Connection:
### Using reference books

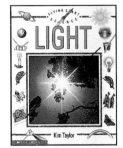

The sun isn't the only source of light in the sky. In fact, the night sky is filled with millions of sources of light. Look at the table you just made. Did you list any natural sources of light that are usually seen at night? If so, what are they?

To find out more about natural light at night, look in the index of *Light*. You'll probably be surprised to discover what some of those night light sources and uses are. Add them to your table, along with any other sources and uses that you think of while you're learning about light.

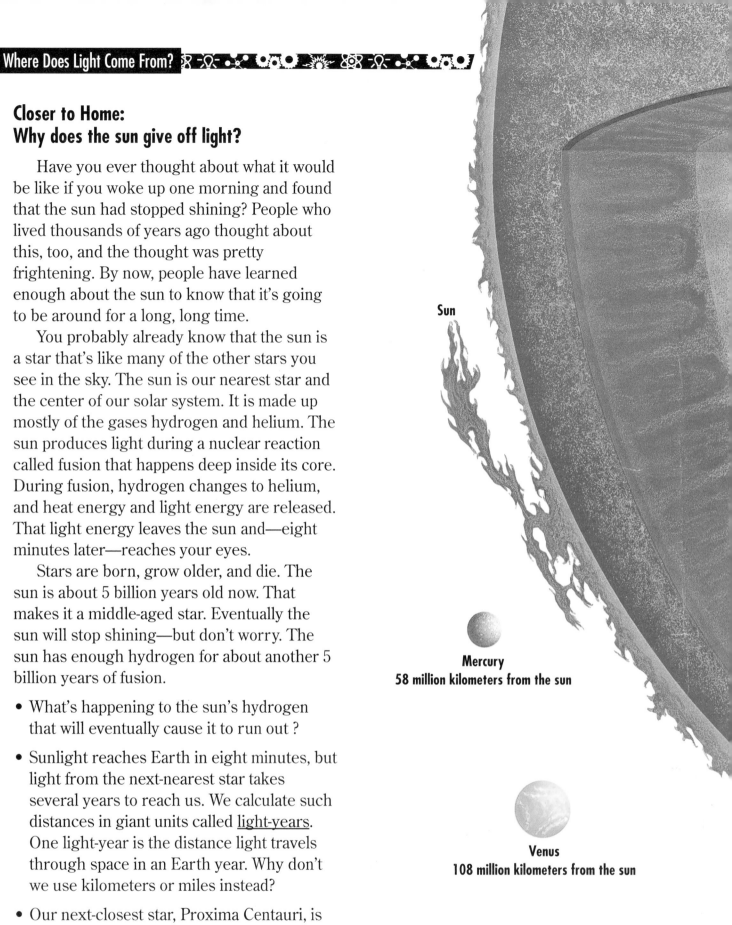

### Closer to Home:
### Why does the sun give off light?

Have you ever thought about what it would be like if you woke up one morning and found that the sun had stopped shining? People who lived thousands of years ago thought about this, too, and the thought was pretty frightening. By now, people have learned enough about the sun to know that it's going to be around for a long, long time.

You probably already know that the sun is a star that's like many of the other stars you see in the sky. The sun is our nearest star and the center of our solar system. It is made up mostly of the gases hydrogen and helium. The sun produces light during a nuclear reaction called fusion that happens deep inside its core. During fusion, hydrogen changes to helium, and heat energy and light energy are released. That light energy leaves the sun and—eight minutes later—reaches your eyes.

Stars are born, grow older, and die. The sun is about 5 billion years old now. That makes it a middle-aged star. Eventually the sun will stop shining—but don't worry. The sun has enough hydrogen for about another 5 billion years of fusion.

- What's happening to the sun's hydrogen that will eventually cause it to run out ?

- Sunlight reaches Earth in eight minutes, but light from the next-nearest star takes several years to reach us. We calculate such distances in giant units called <u>light-years</u>. One light-year is the distance light travels through space in an Earth year. Why don't we use kilometers or miles instead?

- Our next-closest star, Proxima Centauri, is 4.2 light-years away. How long does its light take to reach Earth?

**Sun**

**Mercury**
**58 million kilometers from the sun**

**Venus**
**108 million kilometers from the sun**

 **Earth's moon**

**Earth**
**150 million kilometers from the sun**

# THE SUN'S STRUCTURE

Core of gases

Fusion happens
inside the sun's core.

Energy released
during fusion moves
to the outer layer of
the sun.

Energy from the outer
layer of the sun flows
out into space as
heat and light.

**Think!**

What are the
different ways living
things use sunlight?

▲ The sun is a gigantic
nuclear power plant radiating
energy into space. It takes about eight
minutes for that energy to reach us. How
could you figure out how long the sun's
energy takes to reach Venus or Mercury?

# How Does a Light Source Work?

The sun gives off light energy because it"s so hot. Nuclear fusion deep inside the sun's core produces great amounts of heat energy, and the heat energy makes the sun glow. But what makes a light bulb glow? What makes the bulb in a flashlight light up?

## Exploration:
## Light it up!

**You need:**
Flashlight with batteries
Hand lens
13 cm insulated copper wire
Scissors

❶ Carefully take the flashlight apart to find out how it works. Locate its energy source. Observe its bulb with a hand lens. Make a sketch of the inside of the bulb.

❷ With your scissors, carefully cut off 6 mm of insulation from each end of the two wires.

❸ Place the bulb on the battery so that the bottom of the bulb touches the tip of the battery. Touch one end of the wire to the bottom of the battery.

❹ Touch the other end of the wire to the metal side of the bulb. As soon as the bulb glows, you've completed an electric circuit.

❺ Just barely touch the glowing bulb. What form of energy do you feel? Look at the bulb. What form of energy do you see?

### Interpret your results.

- Chemicals in the battery produce <u>electric</u> <u>energy</u>. How does electric energy get from the battery to the bulb?

- The tiny wires inside the bulb change the electric energy to another kind of energy that you can feel. This kind of energy changes·to light energy. What's the kind of energy you can feel?

- Based on your observations of the sun, the flashlight, and the circuit you made, what do you need to produce light energy?

# HOW A STOVE AND CANDLE CHANGE ENERGY

▲ Electric energy travels through the cord into wires connected to the burner.

▲ The metal burner changes the electric energy to heat energy.

▲ The burner gets so hot that some of the heat energy changes to light.

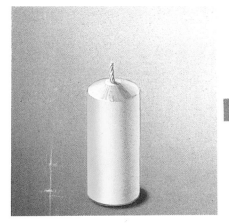

▲ Candle wax can combine with oxygen in the air to release energy.

▲ Adding a small amount of heat energy can ignite a candle wick.

▲ Heat energy makes the candle wax melt. When the wax gets hot enough, it burns and gives off heat and light energy.

## Exploration Connection:
### Interpreting diagrams

Energy is easy to recognize but it's very hard to describe. Scientists say that energy is the ability to change something or to do work. Some objects, such as the battery you used and the candle in the diagram, contain chemicals that can change in ways that release energy. The energy in objects such as the candle and the battery can be used whenever you need it. What else can you think of that contains stored energy? How do you get your energy?

As you can see from the diagram, energy comes in many different forms. Energy can also change from one form to another. If you want to see a quick change of energy, rub your hands together quickly. What kind of energy is produced? How can you tell? **Try it!** Where did you get the energy to move your hands?

Study the diagram. Both the candle and the stove change one form of energy to another. Which device works more like a flashlight works? Explain your choice.

You've discovered how the flashlight produces light. You know how a stove and a candle produce light. You could also produce light energy without using any batteries, wall outlets, bulbs, or fire. How do you think you could do this?

▶ Chemicals mixing together make the glowstick give off light energy.

# Exploration:
## Change some energy.

**You need:**

Wind-up monster
Hand lens

❶ Observe what your monster does by winding it up and putting it on the floor.

❷ Now look inside your monster's mouth to see how it works. Use a hand lens to get a better look.

❸ Make a diagram like the one on page 11 that shows how your monster's energy changes. Start your diagram by showing your hands winding up the monster. Label every part of your diagram. Label the places where energy changes from one form to another.

### Interpret your results.

• How did the monster produce light?

• Why did you have to include your hands in the diagram of your monster's energy changes?

• Think about everything the monster did. What forms of energy were produced?

• Is there anything you could put on your diagram that would go before your hands?

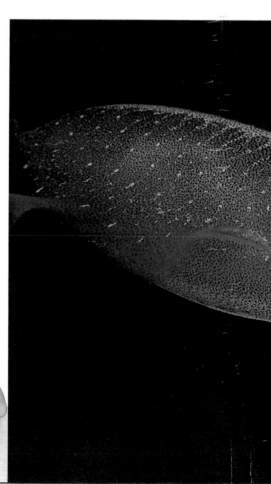

## Closer to Home:
## Things that glow in the dark

You know that the stored chemical energy in a candle can be changed to heat energy and light energy. Animals such as the firefly and the flashlight fish get chemical energy from the food they eat. So do you. The chemical energy stored in your body changes to mechanical energy when you pick up a pencil, walk, or move in any way. Some of the chemical energy stored in your body also changes to heat energy. Feel your partner's forehead for proof. Some of the chemical energy stored in a cuttlefish or a firefly's body changes to mechanical energy and heat energy. Unlike you, they are able to change some of the chemical energy in their bodies into light energy. This change is called bioluminescence.

A light stick glows for a similar reason. It has two chemicals inside it. When you bend the light stick, you can feel a seal between the two chemicals break. Breaking the seal lets the two chemicals mix together. As they mix, they change each other into a new chemical. This change produces light energy. After a while the light stick begins to lose its glowing power.

- How is the way a cuttlefish produces light like the way a flashlight produces light?

- How is it different?

▼ Fireflies are bioluminescent, too. Why do you think bioluminescence is less common among animals that live on land than it is among those that live in the deep ocean?

▼ Cuttlefish can change the color of their skin. Sometimes the change is so fast, they look like waves of colorful designs.

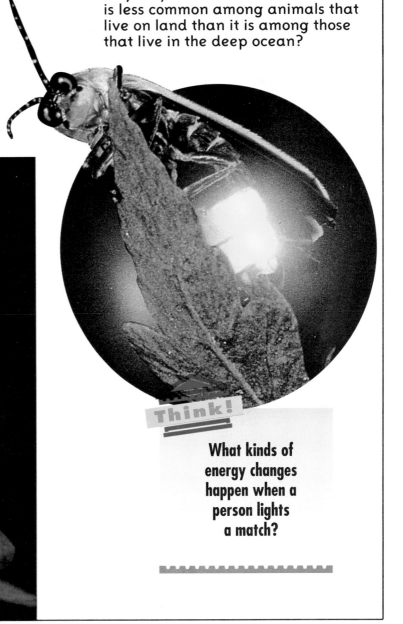

**Think!**

**What kinds of energy changes happen when a person lights a match?**

# What Determines the Brightness of Light?

When you're outside at night, your eyes are bombarded by light coming at you from many different sources. You might see lights of different colors—the three colors in a traffic light, for example. You might also see some lights that appear brighter than others, like the light from a car headlight. But a star actually makes a lot more light than a car headlight does. Why, then, does the headlight appear so much brighter than the star?

## Exploration:
## Compare the brightness of lights.

**You need:**

Aluminum foil
Flashlight
2 "D" batteries
Scissors
Black paper
Tape

❶ Crumple the foil into a mass the size of a battery. Take one of the batteries out of the flashlight and replace it with the foil. Put the flashlight back together.

❷ Cut a piece of black construction paper in a circle a little bigger than the front of the flashlight. Poke a hole in the center of the paper with a pencil. Tape the paper firmly over the front of the flashlight.

❸ Darken the classroom. Have one partner hold the flashlight and switch it on. Take five giant steps away from the light. Then take five more giant steps away. Notice how the light changes as you walk away from it. Take five giant steps back toward the light. Notice how the light changes as you move closer to it.

❹ Turn off the flashlight. Take out the foil and replace it with the other battery.

❺ Repeat steps 2 and 3.

### Interpret your results.

• How did the light appear to change as you moved toward and away from it?

• How did the light appear to change when you put in the second battery? Why?

# HOW BRIGHT IS IT?

▲ The sun at noon on a clear day (10,000 ft-candles)

▲ The lamp by a bed (10 ft-candles)

▲ A streetlight from the sidewalk (1/20 of a ft-candle)

▲ A full moon on a clear night (1/40 of a ft-candle)

## Exploration Connection:
### Interpreting graphs

When you changed the number of batteries in the flashlight you changed the actual <u>brightness</u> of the bulb—the total amount of light it produces. As you walked away from the flashlight you probably noticed that the bulb appeared less bright. That's because rays of light spread out when they leave a source. By the time the light rays reach your eyes, they may not appear to be very bright at all. We measure the "apparent" brightness of a light source in units called foot-candles. The diagram shows some common sources of light and how bright they appear to be at a certain distance. Which light sources could you use for reading this book?

Now look at the graph. The left side of the graph shows the brightness of light coming from a source. The bottom of the graph shows how far from the source a person is. What statement could you make about distance and brightness by looking at the graph? How does the graph compare with what you discovered in the Exploration?

## BRIGHTNESS AND DISTANCE

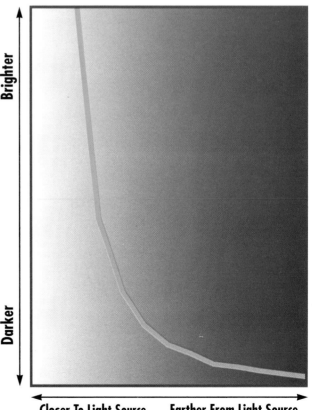

Brighter

Darker

◄ Closer To Light Source   Farther From Light Source ►

15

◄ 60-watt carbon filament bulb— a replica of the one invented by Thomas Edison

▼ 2,000-watt Tungsten element bulb—often used for stage lighting

## Closer to Home:
## Brightness and dollars

Have you ever seen your family's electric bill? It tells the amount of electricity that your family uses in one month. Electric power is measured in units called watts. Large amounts of electricity, such as the amount a family might use in one month, are measured in kilowatt-hours. A kilowatt is 1,000 watts. If your family uses 1 kilowatt of electric power for 1 hour, you've used 1 kilowatt-hour of electrical energy.

Find each place on the picture of the electric bill that refers to kilowatt-hours. How does the electric company use kilowatt-hours to decide how much money this person owes?

Compare the brightness of these light bulbs. Find the number of watts each bulb uses. The wattage of a bulb tells how much electric power it takes to light it. How brightly a bulb of the same type shines depends on the wattage of the bulb. A 100-watt bulb uses ten times as much power as a 10-watt bulb.

• How does the wattage of the bulbs compare with their brightness?

• What could your family do to save money on your electric bill?

▲ 52-watt neon advertising sign

▶18-watt compact flourescent bulb—used for economical lighting in a home or office

**Think!**

There are many stars in our galaxy that are much bigger and brighter than our sun. Why does the sun appear to be much brighter than any other star?

For service and billing information call
212-555-1234

Service to: Jennifer Lyman
at: 3467 Main St.

Your account number
12-3456-7890-0067-8

BILLING DETAIL

ELECTRIC USE - RATE EL1 RESIDENTIAL

10/04/93 reading (Actual)........    6430
09/02/93 reading (Actual)........   -6394
Meter reading difference             36
Meter multiplier                    x10
Total KWH used in 32 days.......    360

CHARGES FOR ELECTRICITY USED

Basic service charge:                    $6.04
(does not include usage)
      KWH        COST/KWH
First 266.7 @ 14.4057¢              38.42
Next   93.3 @ 13.7621¢              12.84
Fuel adjustment @ .5556¢             2.00
Sales tax @ 4.000%                   2.37

CURRENT ELECTRIC CHARGES           $61.67

AVERAGE DAILY ELECTRIC USE

█ = Actual, ▯ = Estimated
▯ = Other Customers This Period

KWH
25
20
15
10
5
O N D J F M A M J J A S O
'92              DAILY AVERAGES        '93

                              KWH
            TEMP.            USED
            DEGREES
THIS PERIOD:   65           11.25
SAME PERIOD
LAST YEAR:     65           10.33

# How Does Light Travel?

You know the way many sources of light work. You also know that when a source—a flashlight, for example—produces light, it takes time for the light to reach your eyes. Light from the flashlight travels along a certain path. What do you think this path is like?

## Exploration:
## Observe the path of light.

**You need:**
Black paper
Scissors
Pencil
Tape
Flashlight
Books
Ruler
Stick

❶ Cut a piece of black construction paper in a circle a little bigger than the front of the flashlight. Poke a tiny hole in the center of the paper with a pencil. Tape the circle over the front of the flashlight so that no light leaks from gaps between the paper and the flashlight.

❷ Work on a table or floor that is next to a wall. Stack a few books. Then place the flashlight on top of the books.

❸ Cut a square of black paper 5 cm on each side. Tape it to the stick.

❹ Put the flashlight on a pile of books 30 cm away from the wall. Aim the light at the wall.

❺ Hold the stick with the cardboard 3 cm away from the wall. Observe the shadow on the wall. Have one of the group members measure the height of the shadow. Record your results.

❻ Now put the flashlight on the books 60 cm away from the wall. Measure the shadow and record its height.

### Interpret your results.

• Draw a diagram that shows how the shadow on the wall was formed. Draw lines to show light's path from the flashlight to the paper square, and from the square to the wall.

• How does the distance of a light source from an object affect the size of a shadow?

▲ This Indonesian shadow puppet is made of flat pieces of paper. It's placed behind a screen and a light source is set behind it.

## Exploration Connection:
### Interpreting diagrams

Sometimes you see an object because it sends out light. Often, however, objects become visible to you when they are struck by light from a source. The light reflects—bounces—off the object into your eye. What path does light take from its source to the object? What path do you think light takes from the object to your eye?

The diagram can help you answer that question. Use your finger to trace the light that comes from the sun and bounces off the tree into each person's eyes. Most often you see objects because they reflect some of the light that strikes them into your eyes. Could the people in the diagram see the car? What does this tell you about the path light travels when it reflects off objects?

Nothing travels straighter or faster than light. And nothing gives you as much instant information about your world. You can learn something from even the tiniest amount of light.

# Exploration:
## Make a pinhole camera.

**You need:**
2 cardboard tubes
2 pieces of black paper
Aluminum foil
2 rubber bands
Pin
Tracing paper
Tape
LabMat 5

❶ Roll up the sheets of black paper and slide one roll into each cardboard tube.

❷ Cover one end of one of the tubes with a piece of foil. Hold it in place with a rubber band. Push the pin into the center of the foil to make a tiny hole.

❸ Cover the other end of the tube with tracing paper, and hold it in place with a rubber band.

❹ Hold the second tube to the tracing-paper end of the first tube. Tape the tubes together. Make sure the tubes are tight so light can't leak in between them.

❺ Take your pinhole camera to the window. Before you look through it, find an object in bright light. Now aim the foil end of your camera at the object, and look at it through the open end of the camera. Make sure to cover the opening around your eye.

❻ Finish the diagram on your LabMat that shows the path that light traveled to form the image in your camera.

### Interpret your results.

• How was the image in your pinhole camera different from the way the object looked without the camera?

• How does your LabMat diagram explain what happened to the image?

• What would happen if you made another pinhole in your camera? **Try it!**

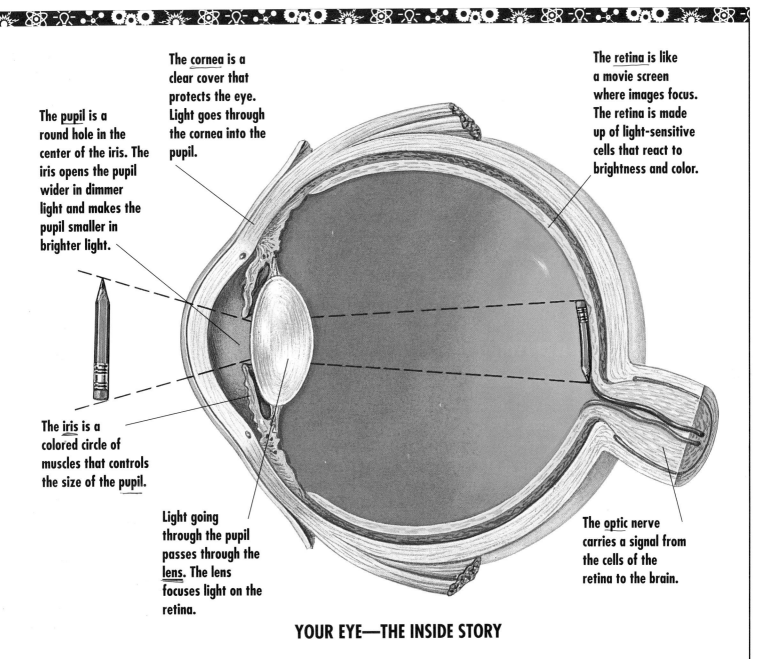

**The pupil** is a round hole in the center of the iris. The iris opens the pupil wider in dimmer light and makes the pupil smaller in brighter light.

**The cornea** is a clear cover that protects the eye. Light goes through the cornea into the pupil.

**The retina** is like a movie screen where images focus. The retina is made up of light-sensitive cells that react to brightness and color.

**The iris** is a colored circle of muscles that controls the size of the pupil.

**Light going** through the pupil passes through the **lens**. The lens focuses light on the retina.

**The optic nerve** carries a signal from the cells of the retina to the brain.

**YOUR EYE—THE INSIDE STORY**

## Closer to Home: The world's best cameras

The pinhole camera you made is actually a model of how light enters your eye. Light reflected from an object travels right into your eyes, just as the light passed through the pinhole in the foil. But what happens to light inside the eye?

Use a finger to trace the path of light from the pencil through each part of the eye. Notice that the image of the pencil is upside down on the retina. The brain uses the nerve signals from the eye to make a right-side-up image of the pencil. If your brain didn't do this, the world would look much like it did through your pinhole camera!

- How is the pupil like the pinhole in your pinhole camera?
- How is the retina like the tracing paper that you used in your pinhole camera?

Even with very bright headlights, people have to drive slowly on curvy and hilly roads at night. Why can't drivers see what's around a curve?

# What Happens When Light Hits a Smooth, Shiny Surface?

When light strikes a tree, a wall, or anything that has a surface that's not smooth, the light is scattered—reflected in many different directions. That's why people in different positions can see the same object. Not all surfaces scatter light, though. What do you think happens to the path of light when it strikes a smooth, shiny surface?

▶ A mirror starts out as ordinary glass.

## Exploration:
## Bounce light off a mirror.

**You need:**
String
Scissors
Adhesive Tape
Pen
Flat Mirror
Folded paper
Ruler
LabMat 6

❶ Cut a 200 cm length of string and mark it every 50 cm with tape. Tape the string to the floor.

❷ Stand with your toes at the end of the string and face the wall. Have your partner tape the mirror to the wall so that you can see the tips of your shoes in the mirror.

❸ Your partner should stand at each mark, hold the folded paper at floor level, and then slowly raise the paper until you can't see your shoes in the mirror. Use string and a ruler to measure the height of the paper. Record the height of the top of the paper at each mark. ✎

❹ Then your partner should stand again at each mark, hold the paper up in the air, and slowly lower it until you can't see your shoes. Record the height of the bottom of the paper at each mark. ✎

❺ After finding the heights, plot them on your LabMat graph. ✎

### Interpret your results.

• How does the angle at which light hits a flat, smooth, shiny surface compare with the angle at which the surface reflects the light back?

• How is the image reflected in a mirror different from the image you saw in your pinhole camera?

## Exploration Connection:
### Using reference books

A mirror isn't the only object that has a smooth, shiny surface. Have you ever seen your face reflected back to you in a puddle of water? Water is clear, so why don't you see only the bottom of a puddle of water when you look into it? To find out more about mirrors, check the index of *Energy and Light*. Then look up the references you find, and draw a diagram that explains how water can be a mirror.

◄ A mixture of silver and other metals is sprayed onto one side of the glass and then hardened in an oven. What do you think the silver mixture does to the glass?

◄ After the mirror is cut to size, its edges are ground smooth for safety.

Mirrors can be tricky. They reflect light at the same angle that the light hits them, but the image in a mirror seems to be reversed. If you part your hair on the right side, your reflection in the bathroom mirror shows the part on the mirror image's left side. **Try it!** If a flat mirror does that to an image, what do you think a curved mirror would do?

# Exploration:
## Investigate curved mirrors.

**You need:**
White paper
Scissors
Ruler
Shiny metal spoon

❶ Cut a strip of paper 15 cm long by 4 cm wide. Draw three lines 1 cm apart from one end of the strip to the other. Draw 14 lines across the strip, 1 cm apart. Cut one end of the paper into a point.

❷ Hold the back of the spoon about 20 cm in front of your face. In your other hand, hold the strip of paper with the point in front of, and almost touching, the spoon. The lines on the paper should be facing the spoon.

❸ Slowly bring the paper strip toward your face without moving the spoon. Observe what happens to the reflection of the paper and the spaces between the lines.

❹ Repeat steps 2 and 3 with the front of the spoon toward you.

### Interpret your results.

• When you moved the paper strip, how did the reflection of the lines on the back of the spoon change? on the front of the spoon?

• How is the image formed in a curved mirror different from the image formed in a flat mirror?

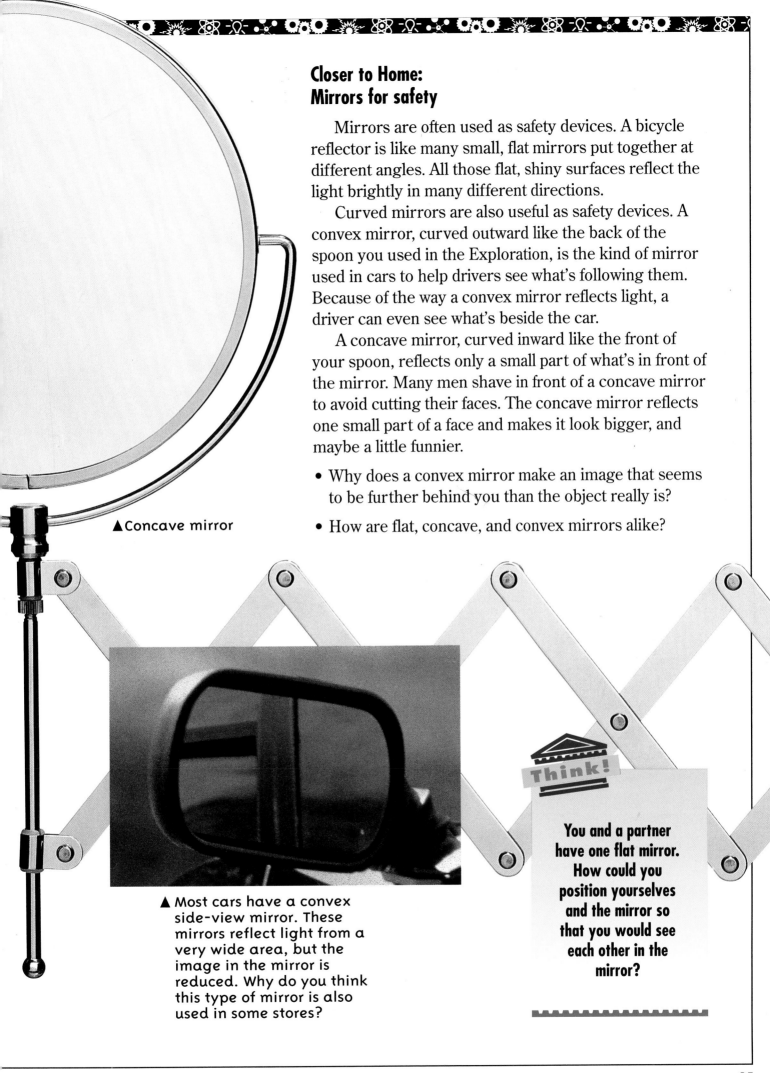

## Closer to Home:
## Mirrors for safety

Mirrors are often used as safety devices. A bicycle reflector is like many small, flat mirrors put together at different angles. All those flat, shiny surfaces reflect the light brightly in many different directions.

Curved mirrors are also useful as safety devices. A convex mirror, curved outward like the back of the spoon you used in the Exploration, is the kind of mirror used in cars to help drivers see what's following them. Because of the way a convex mirror reflects light, a driver can even see what's beside the car.

A concave mirror, curved inward like the front of your spoon, reflects only a small part of what's in front of the mirror. Many men shave in front of a concave mirror to avoid cutting their faces. The concave mirror reflects one small part of a face and makes it look bigger, and maybe a little funnier.

- Why does a convex mirror make an image that seems to be further behind you than the object really is?

- How are flat, concave, and convex mirrors alike?

▲Concave mirror

▲ Most cars have a convex side-view mirror. These mirrors reflect light from a very wide area, but the image in the mirror is reduced. Why do you think this type of mirror is also used in some stores?

**Think!**

You and a partner have one flat mirror. How could you position yourselves and the mirror so that you would see each other in the mirror?

# How Can the Path of Light Be Bent?

Light can be reflected. The path of light can also be bent. Have you ever tried to pick up a coin "from" the bottom of a swimming pool? If you have, you know that it's not as easy as it sounds. You hold your breath, dive in, and reach for the coin—but when you get to the bottom of the pool, the coin isn't where you thought it would be. What do you think is happening?

## Exploration:
### Bend a ray of light.

**You need:**

Coin
Paper cup
Spoon
Water
Clear plastic cup

❶ Put the coin on the bottom of the paper cup. Have your partner sit so that the coin is just out of his or her sight.

❷ Slowly add water to the cup one spoonful at a time. Ask your partner to observe the bottom of the cup but not to tell you what happens.

❸ Change places with your partner. Empty the cup and repeat steps 1 and 2.

❹ Pour the water and the coin into a clear plastic cup. Add more water to the plastic cup until it's half full. Look at the top of the water from the side of the cup. How many coins appear to be in the cup?

### Interpret your results.

• Why couldn't you see all of the bottom of the paper cup in step 1?

• What happened when water was added to the paper cup? Why do you think this happened?

## Exploration Connection:
### Using reference books

Light <u>refracts</u>, or bends, when it passes at an angle from one material to another. You know that light travels at an incredible speed—300 thousand kilometers (186 thousand miles) a second—through empty space. But light doesn't travel quite so quickly through water, glass, or other materials.

Imagine marching arm in arm with three friends on a sandy beach. The four of you are heading towards the ocean—not directly, but at an angle. When the first person enters the water, he or she has to slow down. If you want to keep marching side by side your group will end up walking in a slightly different direction once you've all entered the water. If your "marching band" was a beam of light, you could say that it had been refracted.

Refraction can cause you to see some strange things. Find the six-legged toad in *Light*. How is the toad like the coin in your clear plastic cup?

◄ The path of light is bent several times as it travels from the air into the glass vase, into the water, into the glass, and back into the air. The result is an image that appears to be broken.

Lenses—like the lenses in eyeglasses—are used to refract light in a certain way. Refracting telescopes, magnifying glasses, and microscopes all have lenses that help you see things that are too small or too far away to be seen with just your eyes. Just as concave and convex mirrors reflect light in different ways, concave and convex lenses refract light in different ways.

▲ These steel-framed eyeglasses were made in the 18th century and were very expensive. Few people could afford to wear glasses at that time.

## Exploration:
## Compare lenses.

**You need:**
Convex lens
Concave lens
Flashlight
Measuring tape
Coin

❶ Examine the convex and concave lenses. Feel the middle and the edges of both kinds of lenses. How are the lenses different and alike?

❷ Hold the flashlight as in the picture. Use the convex lens to focus the light from a flashlight onto the tabletop. Focusing the light means moving the lens closer to or further away from a surface until the light is aimed at one spot. This place is called the focus of the lens. Focus the light by raising the lens up or down.

❸ Have a partner measure the distance between the lens and the focus. This distance is called the focal length of the lens. Record this distance.

❹ Now place a coin on your desk, and stand about 60 cm away from it. Close one eye. Place the convex lens directly over the coin and slowly move it towards your eye. Record your observations.

❺ Try to repeat steps 1–4 using the concave lens. Describe what you see.

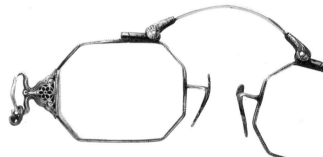

▲ Eyeglasses became much less expensive during the 19th century. How are these 19th-century glasses different from the 18th-century glasses? from glasses today?

### Interpret your results.

• How did the image of the coin change as you moved the convex lens?

• How was the image formed by the concave lens different from the image formed by the convex lens?

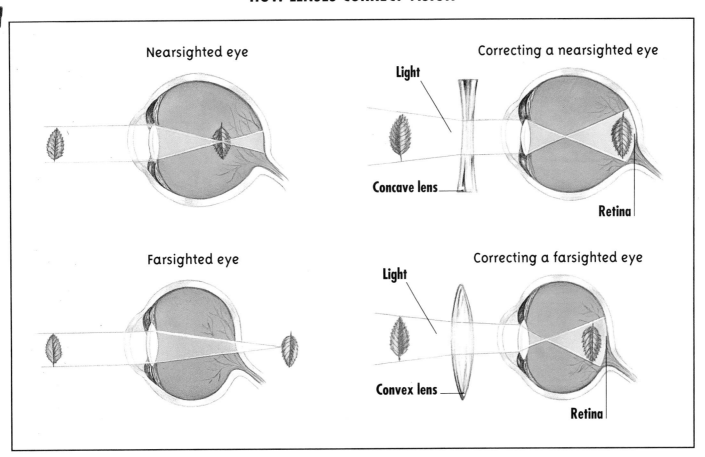

Nearsighted eye

Correcting a nearsighted eye

Light

Concave lens

Retina

Farsighted eye

Correcting a farsighted eye

Light

Convex lens

Retina

## Closer to Home: Seeing clearly

Think of your retina as a movie screen. In order for you to see clearly, the convex lens in your eye must focus light directly onto this screen.

In a farsighted person's eye, the distance between the lens and retina is too short. The lens focuses light from nearby objects behind the retina. A farsighted person sees distant objects clearly, but nearby objects seem fuzzy. Study the diagram. How does wearing glasses with convex lenses help farsighted people?

In a nearsighted person's eye, the distance between the lens and retina is too long. The lens focuses light from distant objects in front of the retina. A nearsighted person sees nearby objects clearly, but distant objects seem fuzzy. How does wearing glasses with concave lenses help nearsighted people?

- Imagine that you have trouble seeing the print on this page. Which kind of lens could help you see the print clearly?

- Imagine that you have trouble seeing people's faces on the other side of the classroom. Which kind of lens could help you see across the room clearly?

**Think!**

**When you're standing up to your waist in water, do your legs appear to be shorter?** Yes

# What's in White Light?

Mirrors reflect light. Lenses refract it. Some materials—or combination of materials—can do both. What do you think happens to a beam of light that's both reflected and refracted?

▲ This prism is a five-sided glass block. Three sides are long rectangles. The two smaller sides are triangles.

## Exploration:
## Separate white light.

**You need:**

Pan
Water
Modeling clay
Mirror
Flashlight
Tape
Paper
Crayons

❶ Place the pan on your desk or the floor about 60 cm from the wall. Fill the pan about 3/4 full of water.

❷ Put a small piece of modeling clay on the bottom edge of the mirror. Then place the mirror in the pan. Lean it against one of the short sides so that the shiny side of the mirror is facing up and towards the wall.

❸ Have your partner hold the flashlight above the pan. Shine the flashlight at an angle into the water so that it reflects off the mirror and onto the wall.

❹ Keep moving the flashlight up and down until an unusual band of light appears on the wall. Tape a piece of white paper to the wall where the light is.

❺ Hold the flashlight so that the image shines on the paper. Then use crayons to make a diagram showing the path that light followed to make the image.

### Interpret your results.

• By placing a mirror in a pan of water, you made a "water-and-mirror prism." How is your drawing of your prism similar to the photograph of the glass prism on this page?

• What does your prism demonstrate about the light that passed through it?

# ELECTROMAGNETIC SPECTRUM

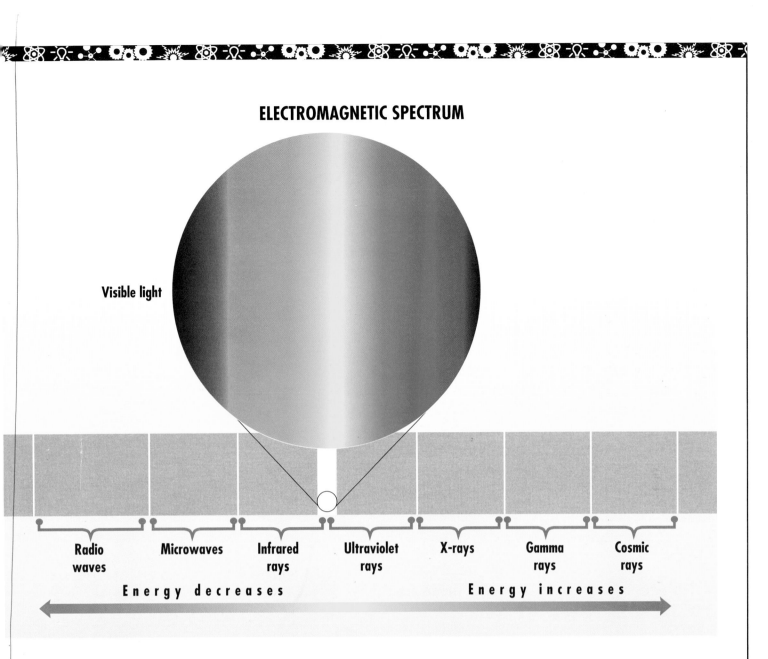

**Visible light**

| Radio waves | Microwaves | Infrared rays | Ultraviolet rays | X-rays | Gamma rays | Cosmic rays |

**Energy decreases**      **Energy increases**

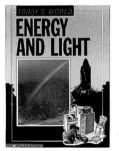

## Exploration Connection:
### Using reference books

The band of light that appeared on your wall is a <u>visible</u> <u>spectrum</u>. You know that light is a form of energy. That band of light on the wall is part of a much larger band of energy called the <u>electromagnetic</u> <u>spectrum</u>. This larger band is shown in the diagram. Which forms of energy shown in the diagram have you heard of before? How are they used?

Can you see radio waves or microwaves? No. Your sense organs don't respond to these parts of the electromagnetic spectrum. The part of the spectrum that you can see is called <u>visible</u> <u>light</u>.

Look again at the spectrum of visible light that you made on your classroom wall. Look around the classroom at all the colors in books, clothes, skin, hair, plants, posters, the walls. Every single color you're seeing is really made up of a combination of the colors in the visible light spectrum.

Humans can see visible light because our eyes have certain cells that are sensitive to light. Can you figure out why we can't see the other forms of energy in the electromagnetic spectrum? Some animals can detect a different part of the electromagnetic spectrum. To find out more, turn to page 22 of *Energy and Light.*

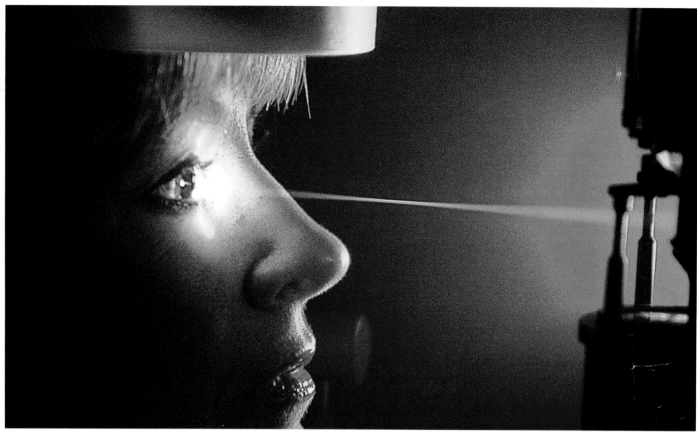

▲ Unlike the light from your flashlight, laser light can be focused into a very narrow beam. The energy from this beam can be used for delicate surgery.

### Closer to Home: Using lasers

How do you listen to your favorite music? Do you use audiocassettes and a tape player? records and a phonograph? Or do you tune your radio to a special place on the electromagnetic spectrum? The chances are, you're now using compact discs, or CD's, for your musical entertainment. The music on a CD reaches your ears in an amazing way. Unlike an audiocassette or a record, nothing touches a CD to produce sound. The CD player uses a beam of laser light to play the music on the disc.

If you look at the surface of a CD under a magnifying lens, you'll see that it's very rough and bumpy—like a messed-up city street or an old country road. When the laser light hits the CD, it reflects off this rough surface and produces a pattern of light pulses that create electric signals. The CD player then turns these electric signals into sound.

**A CD PLAYER**

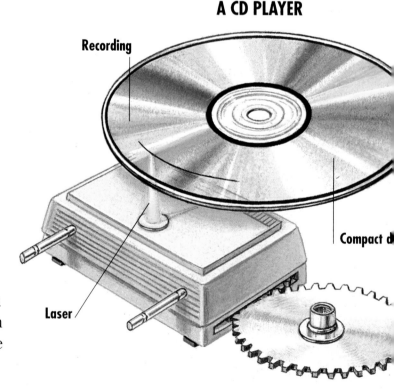

Recording

Compact d

Laser

▲ The concentrated energy of a laser beam can cut through thick steel.

Laser light is made by sending large amounts of energy through certain materials, such as a ruby crystal or neon gas. Unlike the colors of visible light that you see with a prism, all the energy of a laser is concentrated in one color of light.

Do you remember how the brightness of light appeared to change as you walked away from your flashlight? Laser rays don't spread out like the rays of the visible spectrum. Laser rays remain focused in a very narrow beam. That means that their energy stays focused, too. These properties make the laser a useful tool for industry and technology.

Perhaps you've seen a laser light-show at a science museum or on a concert stage. Maybe your school has a laser printer. High-powered laser beams can cut through steel. Laser light beams have even been sent from the earth and reflected off the moon.

The concentrated energy of laser light is also used in surgical procedures to destroy cancer cells or repair delicate tissues. You're going to see more and more uses of laser technology in the future.

- How is producing a laser light similar to producing a spectrum with a prism?

- How is it different?

**Think!**

**The light from your flashlight is made up of many different colors. How do you know this?**

# What Causes Color?

When you look at the clothes that people around you are wearing, you probably see many different colors. You've learned that all these colors are part of the spectrum of visible light. But what is it that lets us see different colors?

## Exploration:
## Make a light theater.

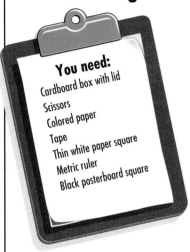

**You need:**
Cardboard box with lid
Scissors
Colored paper
Tape
Thin white paper square
Metric ruler
Black posterboard square

❶ Cut a square light hole about 3 cm by 3 cm in the center of the lid of the box. Carefully poke a small viewing hole in a short side of the box with the scissors.

❷ Cut strips of five or six different colors of paper. Tape the strips to the inside of the box opposite the viewing hole. Don't let the other members of your team see the order that you tape the strips in the box. Record the order from left to right.

❸ Put the lid on the box. Tape the white paper over the hole in the lid. Tape the metric ruler to the lid so that it lines up with one side of the hole, as the picture shows.

❹ Put the black square over the hole with one side pushed against the ruler. Have your partner look through the viewing hole. Slowly uncover the white paper 1 mm at a time.

❺ Tell your partner to name the colors he or she sees as you slowly uncover the white paper. Another partner should record each color and the width of the light hole in millimeters.

### Interpret your results.

• Which colors showed up first for most team members? Which showed up last?

• What did the strips look like before there was enough light to see color?

## WHY YOU SEE DIFFERENT COLORS

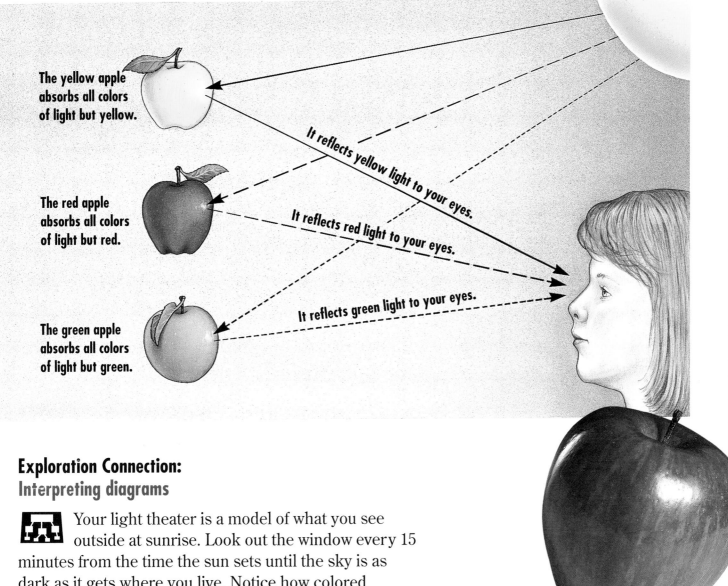

The yellow apple absorbs all colors of light but yellow.

It reflects yellow light to your eyes.

The red apple absorbs all colors of light but red.

It reflects red light to your eyes.

The green apple absorbs all colors of light but green.

It reflects green light to your eyes.

## Exploration Connection:
### Interpreting diagrams

Your light theater is a model of what you see outside at sunrise. Look out the window every 15 minutes from the time the sun sets until the sky is as dark as it gets where you live. Notice how colored objects seem to change. **Try it!**

You discovered with your light theater that you needed more than a small amount of light in order to see different colors. You also learned from working with a glass and mirror prism that all colors of light are mixed together in white light. Look at the diagram. All the colors in white light strike the red apple. The skin of a red apple has substances that absorb all the colors in white light except those that make up dark red. Instead of absorbing the colors in dark red, the apple reflects them into your eyes.

Study the diagram. Which colors does a green apple absorb and reflect? a yellow apple? How about a red shirt? Here's a hard one: What colors does a white shirt absorb and reflect?

▼ This apple is printed with colored ink. Based on the diagram, how are the ink and the light in the classroom interacting?

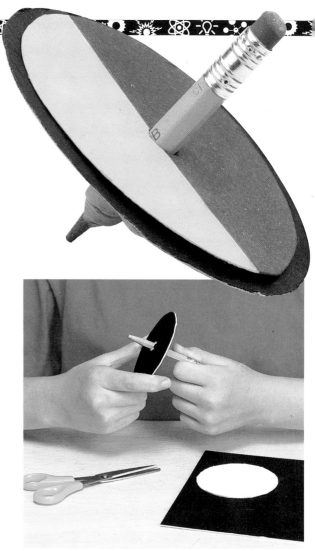

A banana absorbs all the colors of white light except the ones that make that nice shade of banana yellow. The banana reflects those colors into your eyes. Your eyes send signals to your brain, and your brain puts the picture together. What happens when several different colors strike your eyes at the same time?

## Exploration:
## Combine light.

**You need:**
ThinkMat 9
Scissors
Black posterboard
Short pencil
Clay
Red, yellow, green, blue markers

❶ Cut out the ThinkMat circles with scissors. Put a circle on the posterboard, trace around it, and cut out the posterboard circle.

❷ Using the pencil, poke a small hole through the center of the posterboard circle. Push the pencil through the circle until about 2 cm sticks through the other side. You've made a top.

❸ Stick a small lump of clay to the bottom of the circle to give it weight and balance. Spin the top. If it doesn't spin evenly, move the clay around until it does.

❹ Color a paper circle half yellow and half red. Poke a hole in its center. Push the paper circle onto the pencil so that the paper is flat against the circle, colored side up.

❺ Spin the top as fast as you can. What color do you see when the top is spinning? Color and spin other circles with different amounts of red and yellow. Each time you make and spin a different circle, record the results.

❻ Color another circle red and green, put it on your top, and spin it. Color and spin other circles with different amounts of red and green and blue.

### Interpret your results.

• Where does the light reflected by the top come from?

• What color is reflected by the red surface? the yellow surface? the blue surface?

• How did the circles change when you spun them?

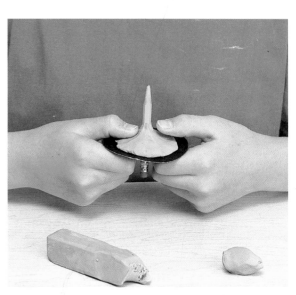

▶ Your eye sees many small dots of color in this painting by French artist Georges Seurat (1859–1891). What will the light reflected by the dots look like if you back away? **Try it!**

## Closer to Home:
## Color vision

What if you suddenly were no longer able to see color? How would you pick out two socks of the same color? How would you know when to stop at a traffic light? How else do people use color?

As you know, the colors you see when you look at an object depend on the colors of light that the object reflects. Whether you are able to tell the difference between colors of reflected light depends on your eyes.

Most people have three types of color receptors, called cones, in their eyes. The three types of cones are most sensitive to three colors of light—red, blue, and green. The signals that cones send to your brain can produce the sensation of every color in white light. Remember what happened when you combined red, green, and blue on your top? Your brain saw something other than red, green, and blue.

Some people have difficulty telling one color from another. This condition is called color blindness.

Most color-blind people can see only blue and red light. Therefore, any color that includes green light is a problem for most color-blind people. Some greens look like reds to them; other greens look like blues.

The smallest pictures show a kind of test used to detect color blindness. What do you see in each one?

- What kinds of problems could a person with color blindness face?

- What would be some solutions to those problems?

▼ **What do you see in each picture?**

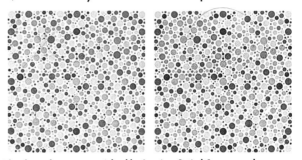

(Detail)

Georges Seurat, 1859–1891, A Sunday on La Grande Jatte—1884, oil on canvas, 1884–86. 207.6 x 308 cm. The Art Institute of Chicago, Helen Birch Bartlett Memorial Collection. © 1993. All rights reserved.

**Think!**

**What color would an object be that doesn't reflect any of the colors in white light?**

# How Else Are Colors Produced?

You now know how light reflecting off an object causes color. However, that's not the only way colors are made. Have you ever seen light coming through a stained glass window? How is the way the window causes colors different from the way the classroom walls cause color?

## Exploration:
### Transmit color.

**You need:**
Red and blue plastic filters
Metric ruler
Scissors
Flashlight
ThinkMat 10
Paste
Posterboard
Tape

❶ Cut a red plastic square 5 cm long on each side. Cut a blue plastic square the same size.

❷ Shine your flashlight onto the back of your ThinkMat. Then hold the red filter in front of the flashlight. Repeat with the blue filter. What shows up on the ThinkMat?

❸ Cut the ThinkMat on the dotted line, and paste the bottom half to the posterboard.

❹ Cut out the parts of the 3-D glasses. Carefully cut out the eyeholes from the center piece.

❺ Tape the red square over the part marked "right eye." Tape the blue square over the part marked "left eye." Tape the earpieces to the glasses. Put the glasses on and look at the next page.

### Interpret your results.

• What colors were in the white light that you shined on the filters?

• What colors of white light did each square <u>transmit</u>, or allow to pass through?

• What colors of white light did the red square absorb? the blue square?

• Instead of changing the color of white light by absorbing part of it and reflecting part of it, how did the plastic squares change the color of white light?

Close your right eye. What's Buzz up to? Now open your right eye and close your left eye. What's she up to now? Keep your left eye closed and read on.

With your left eye closed all the light that goes to your right eye goes through a red filter. It's hard to see a light red object on a white background when you look through this filter. You can see this print because it's blue, but if you open your left eye and close your right eye, this type will disappear. **Try it!** Keep your right eye closed and read on.

You are now looking through a blue filter and you can't see a light blue object on a white background. You can read this type because it's red. Close your left eye and open your right eye and this type will disappear. Now open both eyes and check out the Stegosaurus.

When your right eye and left eye see different images, your brain combines them to make a three-dimensional image. You could make your own 3-D art with red and blue markers. **Try it!**

## Exploration Connection:
### Interpreting diagrams

What goes on behind the scenes when you go to the movies? The person who runs the machines that show the movie loads the movie film into the projector. The projector beams white light onto the film. Huge colored pictures show up on the theater's screen. How does the movie film change the projector's white light into those pictures?

Look at the diagram and the picture of the movie film. Like the squares you used in your 3-D glasses, film is made from a material that lets some light pass through. The yellow parts of the frame transmit yellow—they allow yellow light to pass through. The blue parts transmit blue light, and so on. What color light is transmitted by the black parts?

## HOW A PROJECTOR WORKS

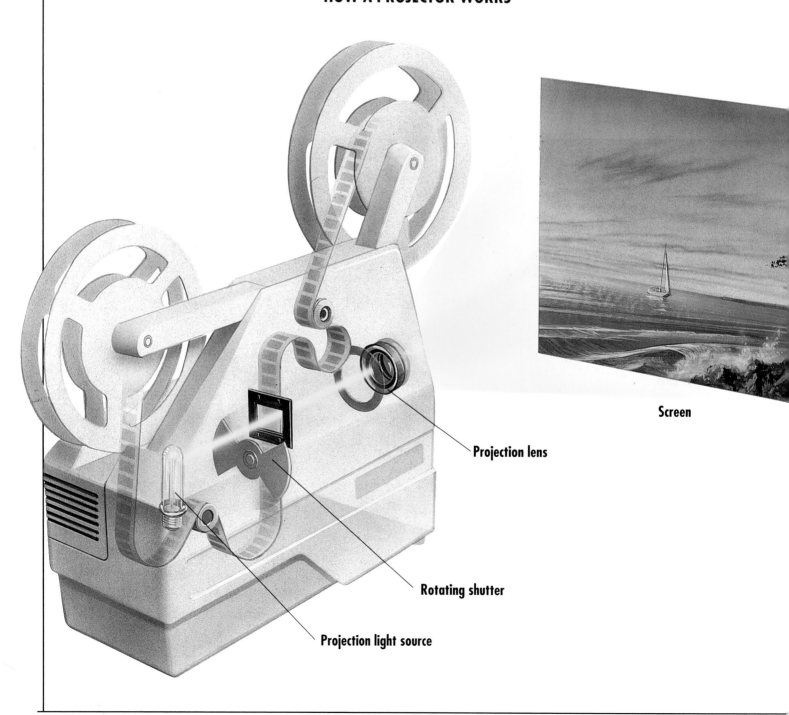

Screen

Projection lens

Rotating shutter

Projection light source

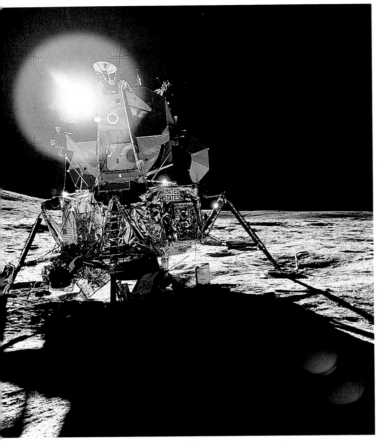

▲ There's no air on the moon, so there are no particles to scatter sunlight.

▲ Air particles scatter sunlight, especially the blue rays.

## Closer to Home:
## Why is the sky blue?

That's one of the first questions very small children ask when they start to talk about the world outside their own home. When you think about how much blue you see because of the sky, and how many days of the year you see all that blue, you'd think most people would know the answer to that question—but most people don't.

The earth's atmosphere—the blanket of air that surrounds the planet—is made up of tiny particles that you can't see. However, these particles have a big effect on sunlight. You know that sunlight is white light, and that white light is actually made up of all the colors of light. The tiny air particles scatter sunlight in all directions. Blue and violet light are scattered the most. Human eyes aren't as sensitive to violet light, so you see mostly the blue light that the air particles scatter.

• How is the way the atmosphere causes the blue color of the sky different from the way the blue plastic square worked?

• How is the way the atmosphere causes blue different from the way a pair of blue jeans causes blue?

**When you put on a pair of blue-tinted glasses, which colors of light reach your eyes? What do the glasses do to the other colors of light?**

# What Happens to Matter That Absorbs Light?

Movie film can be used to project big colorful pictures. Similar film is used to make slides. Although a movie camera and a camera that uses slide film are different in some ways, they have many things in common. Both cameras have lenses similar to the lenses in a human eye. There's no retina in a camera, though. The light that enters a camera strikes the film. What do you think happens then?

## Exploration:
## Make sunprints.

**You need:**

Scissors
Black construction paper
Sunprint paper
Aluminum pan
Tape
Tracing paper
Pencil

❶ Cut a shape from black paper.

❷ Place a piece of sunprint paper, blue side up, on a flat surface. Place the black paper shape you made on the sunprint paper.

❸ Put the papers in bright sunlight for two to five minutes.

❹ Remove the sunprint paper. Put it in the pan of water for one minute. Lay the paper on a flat, smooth surface to dry.

❺ Cut a shape from the tracing paper. Make a sketch on the paper with a pencil.

❻ Repeat steps 2–4 using a fresh sheet of sunprint paper and a tracing-paper shape.

## Interpret your results.

• Objects that don't allow light to shine through, like black paper, are opaque. Objects that let some light through, like tracing paper, are translucent. How are sunprints made by opaque and translucent objects different?

• The sunprint paper is coated with chemicals. What must be true about those chemicals?

## HOW A CAMERA WORKS

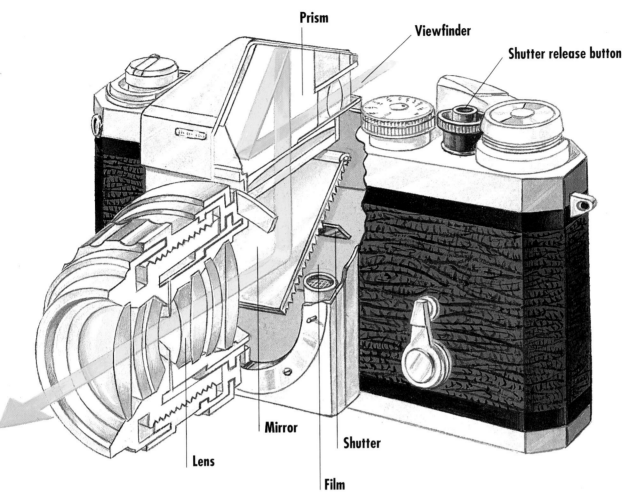

Prism

Viewfinder

Shutter release button

Mirror

Shutter

Lens

Film

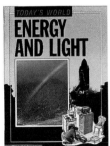

### Exploration Connection:
### Using reference books

The diagram shows how a camera that uses slide film works. With your finger, trace the path of light passing into the camera and out of the viewfinder. Compare the angles at which light hits the mirror and reflects off the mirror onto the prism. Trace the path of light reflected off the faces of the prism through the viewfinder.

If you press the shutter release, the mirror rises and exposes the film to light. Images form on the film when it's exposed to light, just as they did on the sunprint paper in the Exploration. After the roll of film has been exposed, it's soaked in different chemicals to develop the images.

Look at the index of *Energy and Light,* and see if you can find other instruments that use light. Then make a list of all the inventions you can think of that use light in order to function.

▶ After the slide film has been turned into a "positive," it is cut into small pieces and mounted in frames. Why?

Light is amazing. Nothing travels faster or straighter than light. White light contains all the colors of the spectrum. After zipping through a camera, light forms a permanent image on a piece of paper. Film isn't the only thing that reacts with light. <u>Phosphorescent</u> matter also absorbs light and does something unusual with it.

# Exploration:
# Make it glow.

**You need:**

Phosphorescent dinosaur
Cardboard viewing box

❶ Put your plastic dinosaur in a sunny place or under a high-intensity lamp for an hour.

❷ Darken the classroom.

❸ Look at the dinosaur in the dark. What do you see? Where did the dinosaur get its energy? Touch the dinosaur. Is the plastic hot? Record your observations.

❹ Open the curtains, or turn on the lights again. What do you observe?

## Interpret your results.

• Why could you see the plastic object when the classroom was darkened?

• Where did the plastic dinosaur get the energy that enabled you to see it in the dark?

• How could phosphorescent plastic be useful at home? at school? in a movie theater?

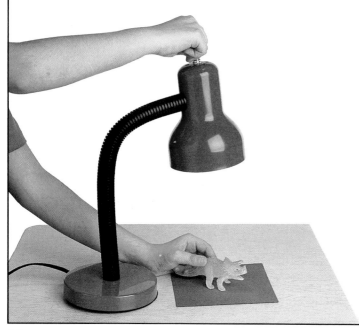

▲ What makes this cyclist safer than many other cyclists?

## Closer to Home: Bicycle safety

Are you a bicycle rider? Do you ride in city traffic or on country roads? Riding a bicycle can sometimes be nerve-wracking—even dangerous. People in cars don't always see the reflectors on your bicycle wheels and pedals.

Certain materials can help protect you when you're riding a bicycle or walking in the dark. Like phosphorescent materials, fluorescent materials absorb light energy and release it, but they release it much faster—almost immediately. Look back at the electromagnetic spectrum on page 31. A fluorescent object absorbs light and gives off light with lower energy. For instance, the pigments in fluorescent paint absorb ultraviolet light and then give off shimmering brilliant colors.

This special property of releasing absorbed light almost immediately makes fluorescent materials very useful for people who ride bikes or walk in the dark. Fluorescent materials make it easier for the driver of a car to see you in the dark and avoid hitting you. Fluorescent stickers can be put on a bicycle helmet. You can wear bands made of fluorescent cloth on your arms and ankles.

- How are fluorescent objects and phosphorescent objects alike? How are they different?

- What are other ways fluorescent materials could be helpful?

**Think!**

**How is the way light changes film in a camera different from the way light changes phosphorescent plastic?**

# How Does Matter Change Light?

You've seen how phosphorescent plastic keeps glowing after it's been exposed to light. You've also seen how light permanently changes photographic film. What do you think happens to the light itself when matter absorbs it? Think about sunlight that comes through a window onto your face. How does your face feel? What do you think has happened to the sunlight that came through the window?

## Exploration:
## Change light energy.

**You need:**
Cardboard box
Black paper
Tape
2 clear plastic cups
Water
Clear plastic wrap
2 tea bags
Clock or watch

❶ Line the inside of the box with black paper. Use tape to hold the sheets of paper in place. Set the box in sunlight, with the open side facing the light source.

❷ Fill both cups with cold water. Put one cup in the box, making sure that no part of the cup is in a shadow. Put one tea bag in the cup. Tape clear plastic wrap over the open end of the box.

❸ Put the other tea bag in the second cup. Place the cup in a place where it gets no direct sunlight.

❹ Observe your two cups once every five minutes for the next hour. Record any changes.

## Interpret your results.

- The device you made is called a <u>solar water heater</u>. *Solar* means "sun-powered." Why is this a good name for the device?

- In which cup did the water heat up? Why?

- You know that a light bulb changes electric energy to light energy. What form of energy does a black surface change light energy to?

- Which do you think would warm up faster during the day, a swimming pool painted black or a pool painted the usual white, green, or blue? Explain your answer.

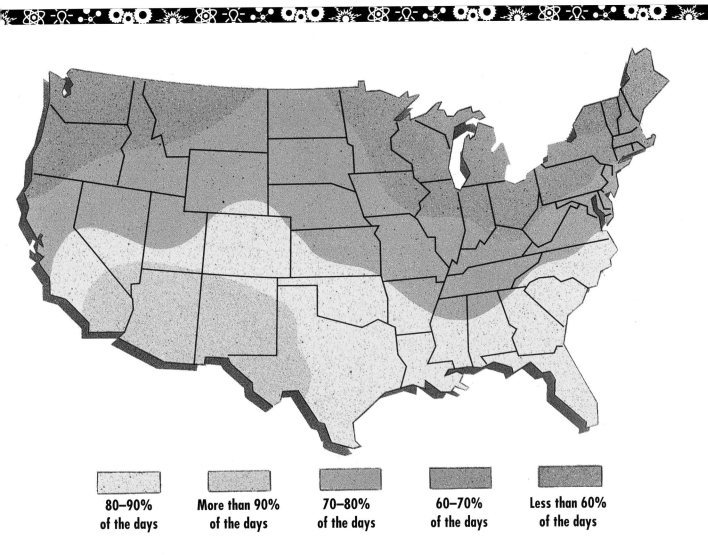

| 80–90% of the days | More than 90% of the days | 70–80% of the days | 60–70% of the days | Less than 60% of the days |

**AVAILABILITY OF DIRECT SOLAR ENERGY IN THE UNITED STATES**

## Exploration Connection:

### Interpreting maps

Solar energy can heat much more water than the amount you put in your cup. In some places, the water in homes, schools, and offices is heated by solar systems similar to the one you made. The picture shows one of these systems.

The amount of heat a solar heater can add to water depends on two things: the size of the heater and the amount of sunlight that reaches the heater. Different places get different amounts of sunlight, and the same place gets different amounts at different times of the year. Because of the earth's shape, some places get much more intense sunlight than other places do.

The map shows how much sunlight different parts of the continental United States receive. Would your community be a good place for solar hot-water heating? Explain why or why not.

▲ The solar panels on this house use light energy from the sun to heat water for an entire family.

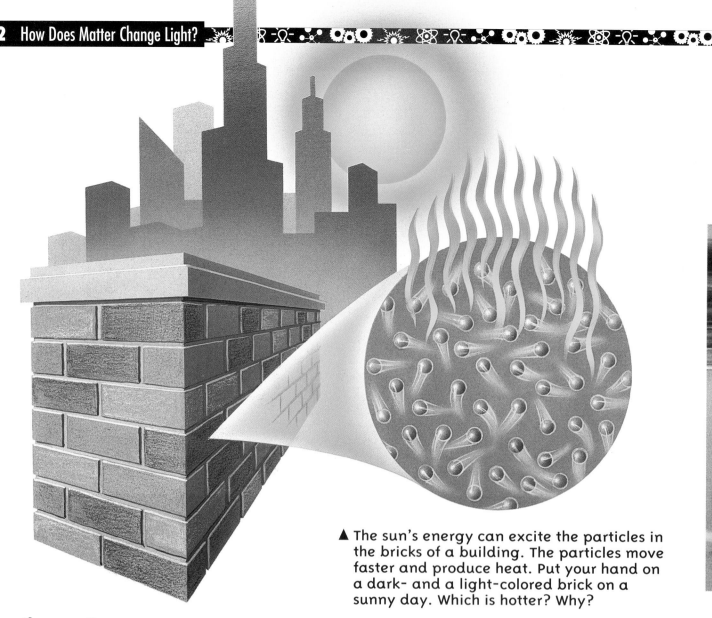

▲ The sun's energy can excite the particles in the bricks of a building. The particles move faster and produce heat. Put your hand on a dark- and a light-colored brick on a sunny day. Which is hotter? Why?

## Closer to Home:
## Sun suffering and sun solutions

Do you live in a city, in a town, or on a farm? Is your home on the coast or far from the nearest ocean? Where you live has a lot to do with the way sunlight changes to heat.

It's hard to stay cool in the city during a summer day. The sidewalks, streets, and buildings are all made of materials that absorb light. All matter—including concrete, tar, and bricks—is made up of tiny particles. When those particles absorb light, they vibrate faster and faster—and that vibrating motion is heat. The faster the vibration, the higher the temperature.

In the summer, especially in areas that get a lot of sun, a city can become unbearably hot. The sidewalks, streets, and buildings change light to heat all day.

Even at night, when you'd expect the air to cool down, a city remains warmer than the open land outside the city. All day long, the buildings, streets, and sidewalks absorb light and change it to heat. All night long, those same buildings, streets, and sidewalks release that heat into the air. You can actually feel a difference in the night air temperature when you go into a large park from an area crowded with buildings.

People can really suffer when there's too much sunlight. On the other hand, people use the sun to solve problems. It's very annoying when batteries go dead in a calculator or a toy. And it's frightening to think about the millions of barrels of oil that are used up every day just to power our automobiles.

► You don't need an electrical outlet to add or subtract with this solar-powered calculator.

▲ High school students built this solar-powered car. They took it to Hawaii and competed with other students. How would this car perform where you live?

Like the solar heater in this lesson, the devices shown on this page change light to other forms of energy. They don't need batteries, gasoline, a wall outlet, or any other source of energy—just light.

- What forms of energy do you think a solar-powered calculator changes light to?

- How many different forms of energy does a solar car change light to? What are they?

- Imagine that you work as a city planner in a city that gets sunlight on more than 90 percent of the days of the year. What recommendations would you make that might help your neighbors stay comfortable?

**Think!**

**Alligators are cold-blooded reptiles. Why do they spend most of the winter days laying motionless in the sun?**

# How Do Plants Change Light?

Solar cars and other machines aren't the only things that change light to another form of energy. So do plants. They combine water, carbon dioxide, and light into sugar, which contains stored chemical energy. When you eat a plant, your body combines material from the plant with oxygen from the air, producing energy. That's the energy your body uses every day. How do you think plants take in light energy?

## Exploration:
## Observe plant pigments.

**You need:**

Small plant
Cardboard viewing box
Red and green filters
Rubber bands
Flashlight

❶ Observe the plant in white light. What color do you see when you look at the plant?

❷ Darken the classroom. Place the plant in the viewing box. Close the lid. Use a rubber band to attach the red filter to the flashlight.

❸ Shine red light on the plant through the hole in the top of the box. Look at the plant through the viewing hole. What color do you see?

❹ Remove the red filter from the flashlight and attach the green one. Shine green light on the plant. Look at the plant. What color do you see?

### Interpret your results.

• What colors of light do you think the plant reflects? How can you tell?

• What happened to the red light?

• How do plants take in light energy?

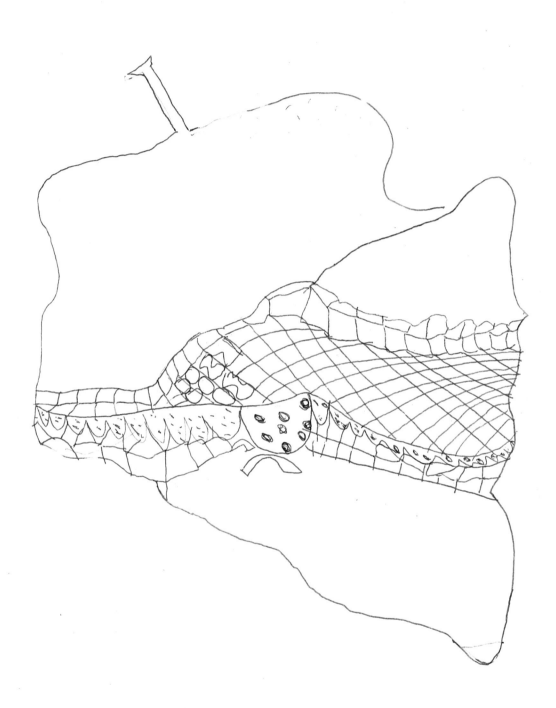

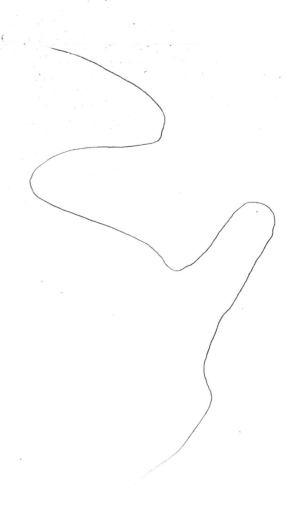

## PHOTOSYNTHESIS

**Sunlight**

Water + Sunlight + Carbon Dioxide → Sugar + Oxygen

**Light energy**

**Water from the ground enters leaf.**

**Sugar leaves leaf.**

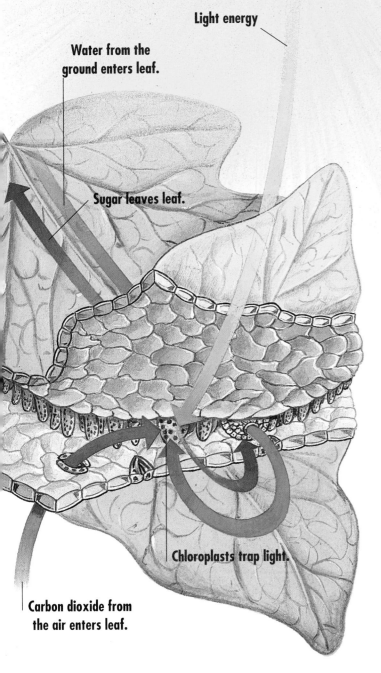

**Chloroplasts trap light.**

**Carbon dioxide from the air enters leaf.**

### Exploration Connection: Using reference books

The food-making process that changes light energy to chemical energy is called <u>photosynthesis</u>. *Photo* means "light"; *synthesis* means "to put together." Certain parts of the plant use light to put carbon dioxide and water together to make sugar. Just exactly what parts of a plant change light energy to another form of energy?

The simplest answer to that question is any green part—but what's special about a green part? Find the close-up view of a leaf cell in the diagram. Inside the cell are parts that look like green jelly beans—the chloroplasts. They are filled with a green substance called chlorophyll.

Chlorophyll reflects the colors of light that make up the particular shade of green that you see when you look at a plant. Different combinations of light cause the many different shades of green among plants. Chlorophyll absorbs other colors in white light. The absorbed light provides the energy the chloroplasts need to make sugar from carbon dioxide and water. The plant uses the energy stored in the sugar to grow, repair damage, reproduce, and do everything else a plant does. To see how else plants use colors, look at pages 26–27 of *Light*. How important is color in the world of plants and insects?

The energy in each
of these foods
started as sunlight.

## Closer to Home:
## Thanks, plants!

Many plants make more sugar than their cells can use. Plants change the extra sugar to starch. Some plants, such as potato plants and carrot plants, store most of the extra starch in their roots. Some plants, such as wheat and oats, store extra starch in their grains. If you let a piece of cracker made from wheat grain dissolve on your tongue, a chemical in your saliva converts part of the starch back to sugar, and you can taste the sweetness. **Try it!**

Plants make enough sugar and starch to feed the rest of the living things on the earth —including humans. Nearly every food chain on the planet begins with plants. Take away the plants and the planet would starve.

When you daydream about food, what do you dream of first? hamburgers? pizza? a great taco? Which of your favorite foods come from plants, and which come from animals?

Pizza crust is a plant product because it's made from wheat; cheese is an animal product because it's made from milk. However, the cow that made the milk that's in the cheese eats plants. Without plants—no cow, no milk, no cheese. No pizza.

Regardless of whether a food is an animal or a plant product, or both, all the energy in any food you eat started as sunlight. Plants change the sun's light into food—stored chemical energy. Animals, in turn, eat plants. Some animals eat other animals, but those other animals eat plants. The sun is the energy source behind photosynthesis, behind plants, and behind animals that eat plants.

- How does a plant grow when it gets very little sunlight? **Try it!** What could people eat in cloudy climates? Where would the energy in those foods come from?

◄The sunnier the weather, the faster this crop will grow. Why?

Every spring, a tree that lost its leaves last fall grows new ones because of sunlight that shone on the tree last summer. Explain.

# How Else Do People Use the Energy From Plants?

▶ Coal-burning power plants generate almost half of the electricity used in the U.S. Where does the energy in the coal come from?

Imagine that you're riding in a car to visit your friend a couple of miles away. Wait! Maybe you're flying in a plane to visit relatives on the other side of the country. Five hours after you take off, the plane rolls down the runway to the airport gate. That night, you sit down to a dinner made in honor of your visit.

Everything you've just imagined uses energy. It takes huge amounts of energy to run airplanes, airports, cars, and homes. Most of the energy people use comes from three fuels found deep below the earth's surface: coal, oil, and natural gas. These fuels have the same original energy source as your string beans and salad—the sun. There's a big difference, however. The plants and animals whose remains became coal, oil, and natural gas have been dead for at least 65 million years! That's why these three fuels are called fossil fuels.

Look at the time line. Just as your school day is divided into periods, geologists—scientists who study the earth's structure—think of the history of the earth as a group of periods, too. By studying rocks and fossils of organisms in earlier periods, geologists have been able to draw conclusions about ways the earth has changed. Those changes include how and where fossil fuels formed.

Oil and natural gas are formed from plankton—floating organisms—that lived in the ocean millions of years ago. As the plankton died, their bodies settled to the ocean floor. Over millions of years, the remains of these organisms were buried under billions of tons of mud and rock. The pressure of the mud and rock and the heat from the earth slowly squeezed and cooked the remains of the organisms into oil and gas.

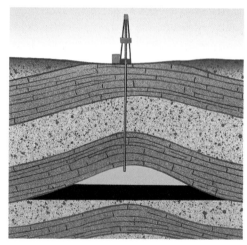

◀ Natural gas is often found near oil deposits. Wells are drilled into the earth to reach both of these fossil fuels.

## GEOLOGICAL TIME

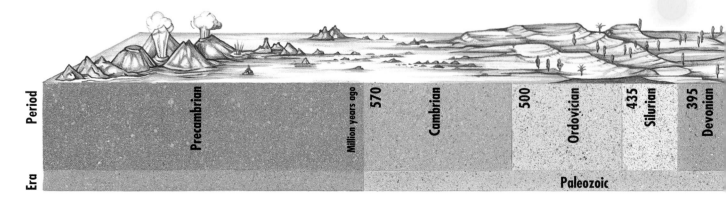

Period

Precambrian

Million years ago 570

Cambrian

500

Ordovician

435 Silurian

395 Devonian

Era

Paleozoic

▼ Some pieces of coal contain clues about their history. This one shows the print of a cycad—a tree that grew millions of years ago.

Coal comes from larger plants that grew in swamps millions of years ago. When these plants died, they fell to the bottom of the swamp. Over millions of years, layers of plant remains settled on top of one another. The pressure of the top layers and the heat of the earth pressed and cooked the plant matter into coal.

Most of the oil and natural gas that people use were formed during the Jurassic, Cretaceous, and early Tertiary periods. Find those periods on the time line. How long ago were they? Coal formed during many different periods, but the biggest and best layers of coal were formed from forests in the swampy river deltas of the Carboniferous period. How long ago was the Carboniferous period?

All the ancient organisms that turned to coal, oil, and gas used energy. The plants—like plants today—changed the energy from sunlight to stored chemical energy in sugar during photosynthesis. The organisms that ate those plants got their energy from the plants—but that energy first came from the sun. No matter where the organisms were in their food chain, all of the energy in the food chain started with sunlight. That energy was stored as chemical energy in the bodies of the organisms, and that chemical energy is still there, even though their bodies have changed to fossil fuels. When people burn fossil fuels, the chemical energy is released and put to work. Fossil fuels represent millions of years of the sun's energy shining down on the earth.

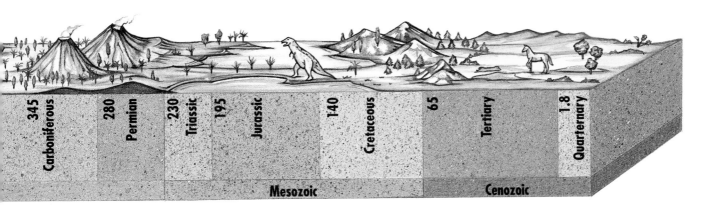

345 Carboniferous
280 Permian
230 Triassic
195 Jurassic
140 Cretaceous
65 Tertiary
1.8 Quarternary

Mesozoic

Cenozoic

## Information Connection:
### Interpreting graphs

It's amazing to consider the amount of time—millions of years—it takes for fossil fuels to form. What's even more amazing is how fast people burn them up.

Until the mid-1800s, most Americans lived on farms and provided many of their own needs. They cut firewood to heat their homes and burned candles or kerosene lamps for light. Farm labor was done by hand or with horses and oxen. The tractor, the automobile, and electric tools hadn't been invented yet.

Today most American families have an automobile. We heat our homes with oil or gas and turn on the TV and the VCR for entertainment. All of these conveniences require energy. Some, such as automobiles, burn up large amounts of fossil fuels when they're used.

Fossil fuels are nonrenewable resources—once people use them up, they're gone forever. The bar graph shows an estimate of how much of each fossil fuel is left in the world. If people keep using oil at the same rate, how much longer will we be able to ride around in cars?

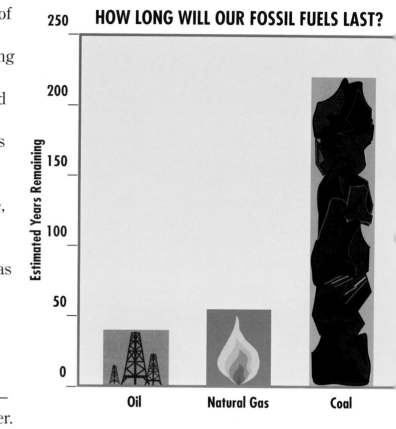

HOW LONG WILL OUR FOSSIL FUELS LAST?

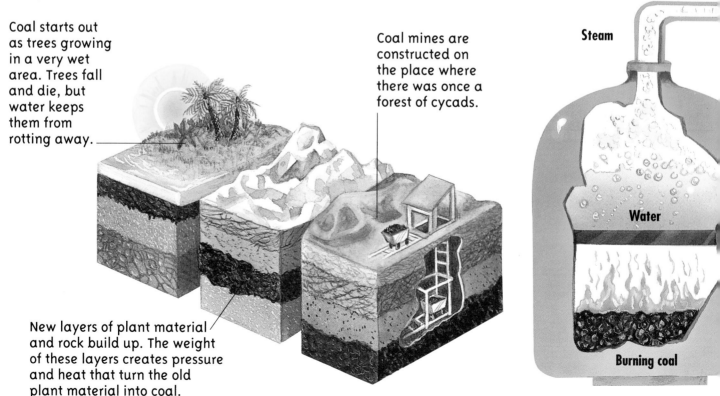

Coal starts out as trees growing in a very wet area. Trees fall and die, but water keeps them from rotting away.

New layers of plant material and rock build up. The weight of these layers creates pressure and heat that turn the old plant material into coal.

Coal mines are constructed on the place where there was once a forest of cycads.

Steam

Water

Burning coal

## Closer to Home:
## Generating electricity

How many ways would your life change if a power outage occurred and the electricity never came on again?

Right now, more than half the power plants in the United States change the chemical energy in fossil fuels to electric energy. The diagram shows how a coal-burning power plant works. Find the turbine on the diagram. A turbine is a group of wheels mounted on a shaft. Each wheel has fanlike blades. In this power plant, the heat from burning coal boils water. The water changes to steam, which pushes the blades and turns the wheels.

As the shaft turns, the magnet on its end turns inside a wire coil. A magnet turning inside a wire coil—or a wire coil turning between magnets—causes the electric current that flows through wires to the electrical circuits of your home and school.

- Where did the energy in coal come from?
- What is a problem with burning fossil fuels to make electrical energy?
- If everyone used less electricity, a lot of fossil fuel could be saved. How can you use less electricity?

# HOW A COAL-FIRED POWER PLANT WORKS

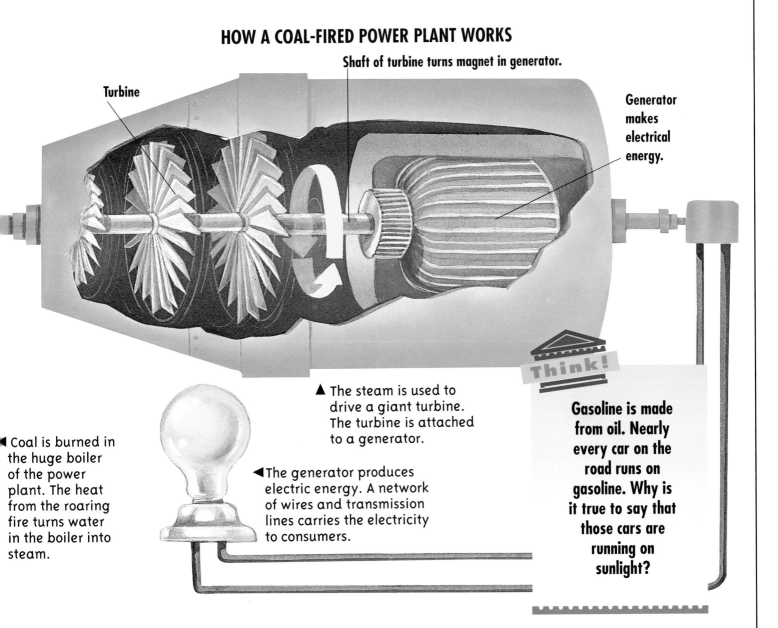

Shaft of turbine turns magnet in generator.

Turbine

Generator makes electrical energy.

◀ Coal is burned in the huge boiler of the power plant. The heat from the roaring fire turns water in the boiler into steam.

▲ The steam is used to drive a giant turbine. The turbine is attached to a generator.

◀ The generator produces electric energy. A network of wires and transmission lines carries the electricity to consumers.

**Think!**

Gasoline is made from oil. Nearly every car on the road runs on gasoline. Why is it true to say that those cars are running on sunlight?

# Identify Problems: Lighting a Space Station

**Think Tank Road Map**

A storm knocks out power to your neighborhood. All you have to do is call the electric company, and a repair crew is on the scene. But how different would this situation be for the crew of a space station? In space, there are no downed wires or overhead power lines to repair.

**15** • In Lesson 15 you'll identify the problems you'd face in designing a lighting system for a space station.

**16** • In Lesson 16 you'll identify some possible solutions to those problems.

**17** • In Lesson 17 you'll make a model of your lighting system, showing the parts of the system and how they work.

 You may also want to review the video.

**Problem:** Your team of engineers has been hired by NASA to invent a lighting system for a space station. Ten people will live on the space station for one year. The station has a control center, a laboratory, crew's quarters, a bathroom, a greenhouse, a small exercise room, and a kitchen/dining space. Your team must put together a plan describing how the station will be powered and how each room will be lit.

⬇ These questions will help you identify the problems you'll face while trying to design a lighting system:

**1** What energy sources will power the lighting system?

**2** How will the parts and equipment for the lighting system be transported into space?

**3** What parts are likely to break down or wear out? Where will replacement parts come from?

**4** What kinds of activities will the ten people in the space station need light for?

**5** What kinds of lighting will be used? Will the same kinds be suitable throughout the station?

**6** Engineers designed lighting systems for each work-space shown in the pictures. What problems did the engineers who worked on these projects have to solve in designing the lighting system of each project?

**Submarine** A submarine carries an energy supply for its lighting system. Most submarines are nuclear powered and don't need any air to work. Why would that be important?

**Antarctica research station** An Argentine research base sits in the remote wilds of Antarctica. It is totally isolated, so how does it get the energy it needs? The small yellow building to the right houses an electric generator that produces energy for the station.

**Underwater research lab**
Underwater habitats are used by some scientists who study the ocean. Most underwater habitats aren't far from land. Cables carry electricity from an energy supply on land to the underwater habitat shown here. Many habitats also have batteries that store enough electricity to run the habitat's light and air systems in an emergency.

Think!

Of the workspaces shown, which one's lighting system is probably the best model for a space station lighting system? Why?

# Find Solutions: Lighting a Space Station

## Solving special lighting problems:

Engineers are called upon to design all kinds of structures, machines, and devices for industry and everyday life. They plan how things like dams and power stations will be constructed and show how the various parts will work.

Until several hundred years ago, most engineers were military or civil. Military engineers designed devices to be used in battle. Civil engineers designed harbors and built bridges and buildings.

Now there are electrical engineers, who may design lighting systems, aerospace engineers, who design spacecraft, mechanical engineers, chemical engineers, and many others.

You've just identified some problems engineers faced in designing lighting systems for unusual work spaces. Now take a closer look at one of them—a submarine. Thinking about how engineers lit an underwater vessel might help you and your team find solutions to lighting a space station.

**1**

Make a chart of the problems you listed in the last lesson. Beside each of your problems, try to list a similar problem the lighting engineers for the submarine had to face.

**2**

Study the diagram of the submarine. Where is its power source located? What are all the spaces that need lighting? A submarine spends months at a time below the surface of the water. How does this affect the type of lighting a submarine needs? What are some special problems that might occur? Below each submarine lighting problem on your chart, record any solutions you find. Could you use any of their solutions for your problems?

**3**

Think about the batteries you've been using as you worked on this unit. Are they as powerful now as they were at the beginning of the unit? Could the same type of battery be used on a submarine? How about on a space station?

**4**

Below each of the space station lighting problems on your chart, record any solutions you can think of. If you have more than one solution to a problem, record them all. You can use both words and pictures.

# SUBMARINE DESIGN

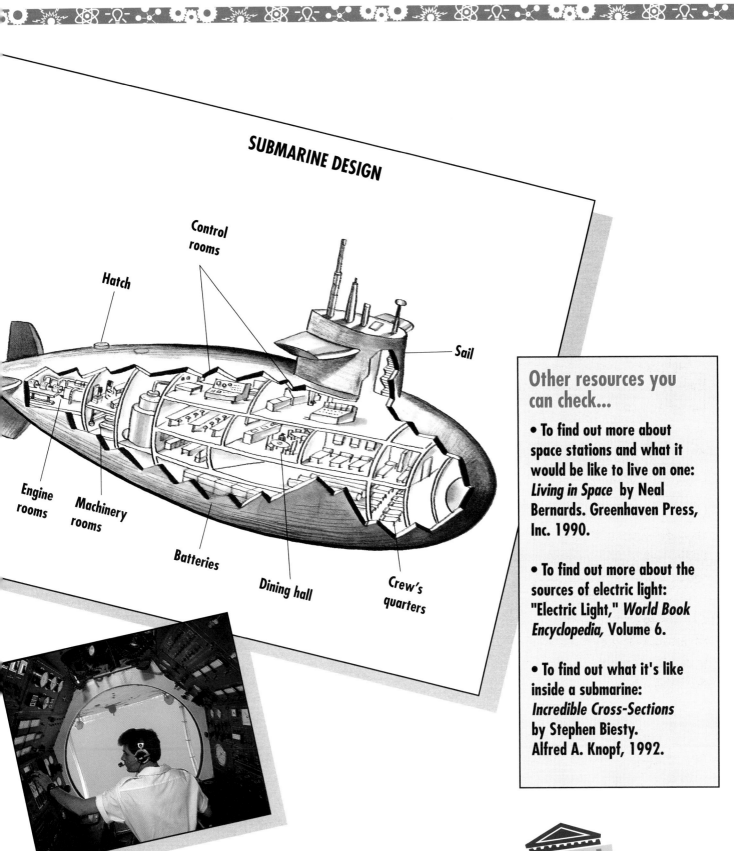

**Control rooms**

**Hatch**

**Sail**

**Engine rooms**

**Machinery rooms**

**Batteries**

**Dining hall**

**Crew's quarters**

▲ **Passenger sub in the Grand Cayman Islands** Strategic lighting allows the engineer to operate the submerging controls of this submarine.

## Other resources you can check...

• To find out more about space stations and what it would be like to live on one: *Living in Space* by Neal Bernards. Greenhaven Press, Inc. 1990.

• To find out more about the sources of electric light: "Electric Light," *World Book Encyclopedia*, Volume 6.

• To find out what it's like inside a submarine: *Incredible Cross-Sections* by Stephen Biesty. Alfred A. Knopf, 1992.

**Think!**

**How does learning about the ways engineers have solved other lighting problems help you with your problems?**

# Make Models: Lighting a Space Station

Your team has identified problems you'll face in designing a lighting system. You've also identified possible solutions to some of those problems. Now it's time to put your solutions to work.

## Possible models for your lighting system:

**Diagram** Use the diagrams in lessons 16 and 17 to help you draw a large diagram of your lighting system. Be sure to label the diagram to show your solutions.

**3-Dimensional Model** Use cardboard, plastic, or any combination of items to build a model showing a space station and its lighting system.

**Written Description** Write a report that carefully describes every detail of the lighting system you've designed for the space station.

**Computer Graphics** Use a graphics program to design a lighting system on the computer.

**Oral Presentation** Give a speech about your lighting system as though your team were making a presentation to NASA's aerospace engineers.

**1**

Study the diagram. How does the structure of each area in the space station determine the type of lighting you will use? What part of the space station will supply electricity for your lighting system? What source of energy is most easily available to a space station?

**2**

Work with your team to design a lighting system. List all the things your lighting system should have. Make sure your design includes these things.

**3**

Make a model based on your design. Choose one of the models you think will work best for showing your lighting system. Gather the materials you need and start working.

**4**

Look at all the models your class has made. How did different teams solve problems? Did everybody think of the same problems? the same solutions?

**5**

How would your models have been different if you hadn't learned how light sources work, how light travels from its source, and what determines a light's brightness? What were the most important things you learned in this unit that helped you design a lighting system?

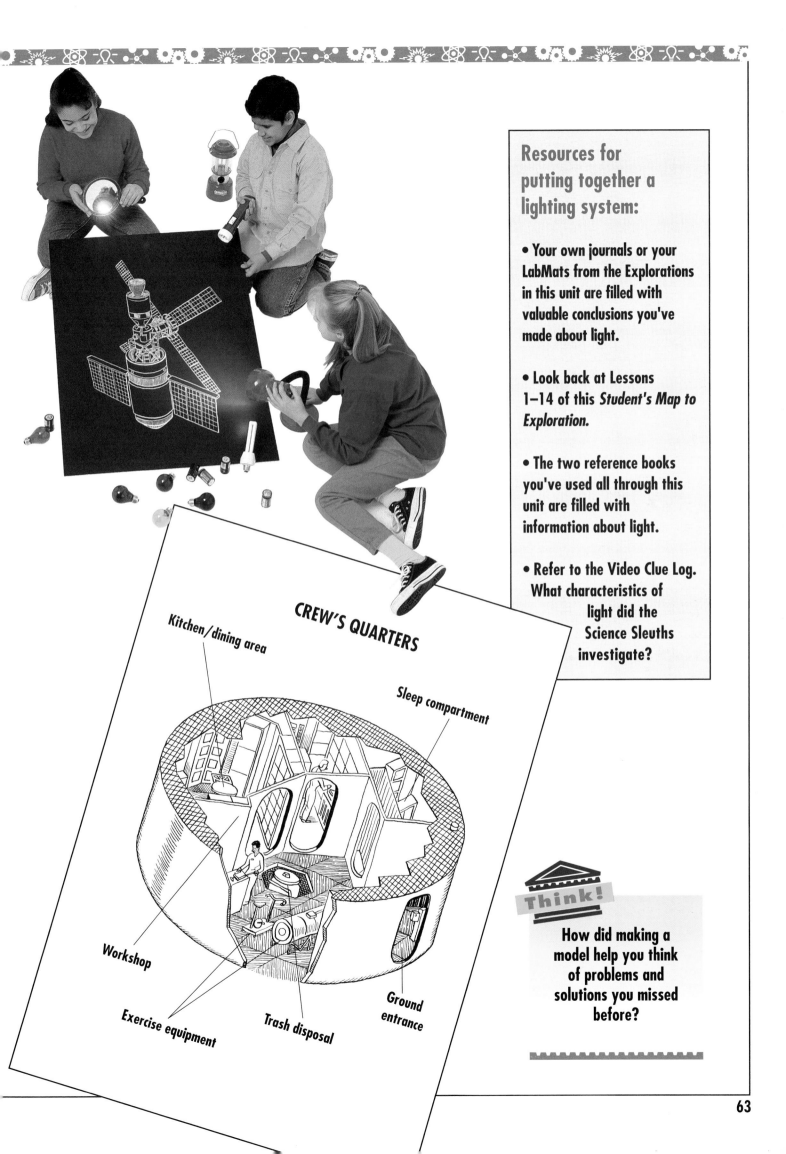

**CREW'S QUARTERS**

Kitchen/dining area

Sleep compartment

Workshop

Exercise equipment

Trash disposal

Ground entrance

**Think!**

How did making a model help you think of problems and solutions you missed before?

# FOR SCIENCE BROWSERS

All articles reprinted with permission.

## The Blink of an Eye

by Steve Charles and Staff
from *Child Life*

**H**ow much can happen in the blink of an eye?

There's a doctor in Missouri who says a lot more happens when you blink than you would think. In fact, you do think. When your eyes are open, he says, they are just soaking up light like a sponge. Your brain doesn't really work too much.

But when you blink, your brain gets to serious work. It analyzes what your eyes have just seen. Then it stores the sight in your memory. That all takes place in a split second—the blink of an eye. You need to blink to think, the doctor says.

Test the doctor's theory yourself. Try some activity, such as playing a video game, that moves very fast. Your eyes will hardly blink at all. That's because you need to see and react. Thinking isn't very important for this. Then read a book. You will blink much more often, because you have to think more! — *September, 1990*

# A Brighter Idea

### from *SuperScience® Blue*

**REGULAR BULB**

**1. A** *filament* **(metal thread) heats up and glows.**

**2. Gas inside the bulb keeps the filament burning evenly.**

**E-LAMP**

**1. A coiled** *antenna* **(an-TEN-ah) gives off radio waves.**

**2. The radio waves vibrate the gas in the bulb. That makes the gas give off light that's invisible to humans.**

**3. The coating on the bulb turns invisible light into a light you can see.**

**Very Fast, for a Human on Earth**
If he ran at top speed for one second, Carl Lewis would go about 41 feet. Measure 41 feet in a hallway or outside to see just how far this is. Light travels much faster. In one second, it would travel about 186,000 miles. That's three-fourths of the way to the moon!

Turning on a light may soon be a lot healthier—for the planet that is. For 113 years, most people have been using the same kind of light bulb that was invented by Thomas Edison.

But now there's the E-Lamp—a bulb that uses radio waves. It lasts a long time—14 years. Compare that to a regular bulb, which has to be changed every 6–12 months. Plus radio-wave bulbs like the E-Lamp use less energy than regular bulbs. In fact, replacing just one regular bulb with an E-Lamp would save 143 pounds (64 kg) of power plant pollution each year.

The new radio-wave light bulbs should be out next year. How much will they cost? Probably about $15. That's 20 times more expensive than a regular light bulb. But because the new bulbs use less electricity and last so long, they're cheaper in the long run. How much cheaper? An old bulb costs about 30¢ a week to keep lit 4 hours a day. An E-Lamp? Only 9¢.
— *October, 1992* 💡

©1994 Peter Menzel

# What's Happening?

by Carolyn Duckworth
from *Ranger Rick*

### Clean solar and electric cars—can they really replace our dirty gas guzzlers?

**O**ur cars are bad news for the environment. They burn lots of gas, and that makes our air dirty. The *good* news is that better cars are on the way. By the time you are ready to drive, you may be behind the wheel of an *electric* car. It may even use the sun to run.

## Racing With Sun Power

Electric cars use electricity to power their motors. These cars usually get their electricity by being plugged into an electric socket. The electricity is then stored in batteries and is used to run the car later.

*Solar* cars get their power from the sun. They use *solar cells* to turn sunlight into electricity. This power can be used right away or stored in batteries.

One of the most radical solar cars was made by a big car company. *Sunraycer* won a long race across Australia. This car crossed the finish line 600 miles (965 km) and two days ahead of all the other solar cars.

*Sunraycer* was a great car for a race. But no one has made a solar car that works well for everyday use. The solar cells are costly and the batteries can be bulky.

Still, Sunraycer gave engineers lots of ideas for building other kinds of electric cars. Now the big car companies are hard at work trying to build electric cars that we all can use.

## Mini Solar Cars

Kids in middle school (7th and 8th grade) can get into solar car racing too. They can enter the "Junior Solar Sprint." These model car races are sponsored by the Argonne National Laboratory and the U.S. Department of Energy. Local races are held each spring, and the national race is in July.

Each model car has to use the same size motor and solar panel. But the kids can build the rest of the car with whatever stuff they want—from aluminum cans to balsa wood to drinking straws!

All of the cars run two races that are 65 feet (20 m) long. The cars are also judged on their *design* (how well they are built).

The first Solar Sprint was held last year, and the second Solar Sprint is going on now. Hundreds of kids around the country entered their cars in local races this spring. The winners will be competing in the national race during July in Washington, D.C.

## Aloha Solar

In 1989, Hawaii had its own solar car race for students in middle school and high school. Those kids didn't build small models—they had to build full-sized cars! And students from Naalehu (Nah-ah-LAY-hoo) School won first prize.

Each group that entered the race had the same amount of money to spend. And they used the same kind of motor and solar panels. Then the teams ran their cars in an uphill race, a short race, and a long race. They were also judged on their design.

The Naalehu School winners got a chance to drive their solar car on a racetrack in Indianapolis, Indiana. (A famous car race—the Indy 500—is run there each May.) Their car wouldn't have won against the gas-guzzling super-speedy cars that usually race there. But it did win an award from the U.S. government—it was named the "Energy Project of the Year."
—*July, 1992*

## Spy Eyes

A dragonfly can see better than any other insect. Each huge, half-circle eye is made up of up to 28,000 little eyes. Dragonflies can spot moving insects up to 40 feet (12m) away.

## Built-in Sunscreen

Hippos have special glands under their skin. These glands ooze out a pink liquid that dries to a hard crust. The crust acts like a sunscreen, blocking many of the sun's burning rays.

**Why Does the Sun Appear Red Sometimes?** Sunlight reaches us only after passing through the atmosphere— a layer of air around the earth. In the morning, the sun's light has to pass through a lot of the atmosphere before we see it. Dust and water droplets stop a lot of its light, so the sun looks darker, or red.

# Hubble Out of Trouble

### by Michael D. Lemonick
### from *Time*

Shortly after midnight on Dec. 18, just five days after the shuttle *Endeavour* returned from the daring mission to repair the Hubble telescope, scientists secretly put the refurbished instrument to its first test. They ordered the Hubble to point toward a bright star and beam its image to Earth. Anxiously, they crowded around a computer screen at the Space Telescope Science Institute in Baltimore, Maryland, as they waited for the picture to appear. The *Endeavour* astronauts had installed the telescope's corrective lenses and other equipment perfectly. But it wasn't certain that the devices would actually work. As the star's image came up on the screen, the scientists stared for a second— then burst into cheers. The Hubble, hobbled for nearly four years by an improperly ground mirror, was going to be as good as new.

In fact, said NASA administrator Daniel Goldin, presenting the first images from the born-again telescope at a press conference last week, "it's better than new. The telescope now gathers light four times as efficiently as it did before the repairs." Its eyesight is so sharp, say scientists, that if it were sitting in Washington, it could spot a firefly in Tokyo.

That's not hard to believe, considering the before and after pictures NASA unveiled. Blurred blobs have turned into sharp, clean images of galaxies, supernovas and stars. But, says senior project scientist David Leckrone, "these are the very first test images. We're not pushing the telescope to its limits yet." As they do, scientists will almost certainly be able to start solving some of astronomy's greatest mysteries: How old is the universe? Do giant black holes lurk at the cores of galaxies? How did the galaxies get formed? Are there planets circling other stars?
— *January, 1994.*

**Before repair**

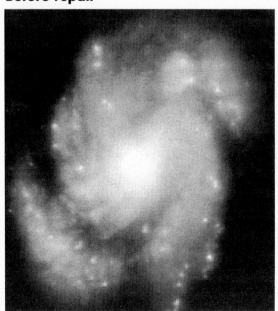

**After repair**

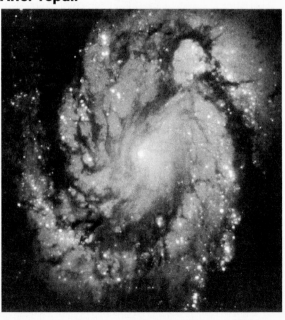

AP/Wide World Photos

# What's a Light Year?

**by Lorraine Hopping Egan**
from *Kids Discover: Light*

The nearest star (besides our sun) is Proxima Centauri. It's 24,813,600,000,000 miles away, give or take a couple of billion miles. That number is clearly too large to handle. So instead of miles, astronomers use light years. A light year is the distance light travels in a year. Proxima Centauri is a mere 4.22 light years away, a much more neighborly number. In one second, a light beam in space would travel 46,000 miles farther than a light beam underwater. That's about two times around the equator.
— *October, 1993* -🔆-

---

# Ask a Scientist

**by Michael J. Klein**
from *The Planetary Report*

**W**hy is space dark when the Sun is shining?

We see things either by direct or reflected light. A lightbulb, or the Sun, appears bright because it gives off light which then travels directly to our eyes. We see a book, or the Moon, by light that it reflects to our eyes. With the Moon, we see light from the Sun that is reflected off the Moon's surface.

When we look at a blue sky, we are actually seeing light from the Sun that has been reflected, or "scattered," by the molecules and dust in Earth's atmosphere. (When we see a beam of light come through a window, we are seeing the light reflected from dust particles in the air.)

In all cases, the light either comes to our eyes directly from its sources or it is reflected to our eyes by some object. Space is dark, even though stars are shining, because nothing there reflects enough light to our eyes.

But space is not empty. Astronomers have long recognized clouds of dust and gas between the stars. These clouds are so far from any star that the light they reflect is just not enough to register on our eyes. We need large telescopes to see these clouds of dust, and even then they are recognized more often by what they obscure than by reflected light. —*Lee Samuel Finn, California Institute of Technology*
— *February, 1987* -🔆-

**Heat in the Sky**
A flash of lightning makes the air around it so hot that the air itself glows.

# GLOSSARY

## Concept vocabulary and other technical terms

**brightness** [brīt´•nis]: *n.* The total amount of light.

**concave** [kon´•kāv´]: *adj.* Hollow and curving inward.

**cones** [kōns]: *n.* The three types of color receptors in the eye.

**convex** [kon•veks´]: *adj.* Curving outward.

**electric circuit** [i•lek´•trik sur´•kit]: *n.* The path of travel for an electric current.

**electric energy** [i•lek´•trik en´•ər•jē]: *n.* The energy created by a flow of electrons.

**electromagnetic spectrum** [i•lek´•tro•mag•net´•ik spek´•trəm]: *n.* All bands of light and lightlike energy.

**energy** [en´•ər•jē]: *n.* The ability to change something or do work.

**fluorescent** [fluər•es´•ənt]: *adj.* Absorbing light energy and then releasing it almost immediately.

**laser light** [lā´•zər līt]: *n.* A very intense beam of light of one color made by putting energy into a material.

**lens** [lenz]: *n.* 1. A piece of glass that refracts light; 2. A transparent part of the eye that focuses an image on the retina.

**light** [līt]: *n.* A form of energy that stimulates the eye and makes it possible to see things.

**light-year** [līt•yir´]: *n.* The distance light travels in one year.

**opaque** [ō•pāk´]: *adj.* Not allowing light to pass through.

**phosphorescent** [fos´•fə•res´•ənt]: *adj.* Glowing after the light source has been removed.

**photosynthesis** [fōt´•ō•sin´•thə•sis]: *n.* The food-making process that plants use to change light energy to chemical energy.

**prism** [priz´•əm]: *n.* A block of glass or plastic that separates white light into the colors of the visible spectrum.

**reflect** [ri•flekt´]: *v.* To throw or bounce back.

**refract** [ri•frakt´]: *v.* To cause a change in direction of a ray of light so that it appears to bend.

**retina** [ret´•ən•ə]: *n.* The layer of cells at the back of the eyeball that is sensitive to light.

**solar water heater** [sō´•lər wot´•ər het´•ər]: *n.* A water heater powered by energy from the sun.

**transmit** [trans•mit´]: *v.* To allow to pass through.

**translucent** [trans•loōs`•ənt]: *adj.* Allowing light, but not images, to pass through.

**visible light** [viz´•ə•bəl līt]: *n.* Any part of the electromagnetic spectrum visible to the human eye.

**visible spectrum** [viz´•ə•bəl spek´•trəm]: *n.* The bands of colored light that appear when white light is passed through a prism.

| | | | | | |
|---|---|---|---|---|---|
| a | add, map | i | it, give | u | up, done |
| ā | ace, rate | ī | ice, write | yōō | fuse, few |
| â(r) | care, air | o | odd, hot | û(r) | burn, term |
| ä | palm, father | ō | open, so | ə | *a* in *above* *e* in *sicken* |
| e | end, pet | ô | order, jaw | | |
| ē | equal, tree | ōō | pool, food | | |